Competency-Based Education

Competency-Based Education

A New Architecture for K–12 Schooling

ROSE L. COLBY

HARVARD EDUCATION PRESS

Cambridge, Massachusetts

Second Printing, 2018

Paperback ISBN 978-1-68253-100-6
Library Edition ISBN 978-1-68253-101-3

Library of Congress Cataloging-in-Publication Data
Names: Colby, Rose, author.
Title: Competency-based education : a new architecture for K-12 schooling /
    Rose L. Colby.
Description: Cambridge, Massachusetts : Harvard Education Press, [2017] |
    Includes bibliographical references and index.
Identifiers: LCCN 2017024022| ISBN 9781682531006 (pbk.) |
    ISBN 9781682531013 (library edition)
Subjects: LCSH: Competency-based education—United States. |
    Education—Standards—United States. | Educational change—United States. |
    Education and state—United States. | Public schools—United States.
Classification: LCC LC1032 .C64 2017 | DDC 371.26—dc23
LC record available at https://lccn.loc.gov/2017024022

Published by Harvard Education Press,
an imprint of the Harvard Education Publishing Group

Harvard Education Press
8 Story Street
Cambridge, MA 02138

Cover Design: Endpaper Studio
Cover Image: iStock.com/traffic_analyzer

The typefaces used in this book are Adobe Garamond, HeronSans, and Roboto.

To our granddaughters, Violet and Ruby Scheer, and our new grandson, Leo Colby Isola. Our hopes and aspirations for their future lie in an education system that will nurture and grow their talents while demanding of them a level of excellence and achievement that will pave the way for whatever path their life's journey will take them.

And to the many school leaders and educators who helped shape my thinking in designing the architecture for competency-based learning, assessment, and grading. Their courage and passion have moved our profession forward into new thinking about teaching and learning.

Contents

Preface

We are called to be architects of the future, not its victims.

—R. BUCKMINSTER FULLER

AS WE CHUG OUR WAY into the twenty-first century, we wonder what happened to all the hopes and aspirations we had for truly preparing our students for the twenty-first century. Education in most of our schools looks nearly the same as it did in 2000, 1990, or even 1980. However, a growing number of teachers and leaders recognize that the one-size-fits-all industrial model of teaching and learning has not met the needs of their students. These educators have, in fact, become the new architects of the future of teaching and learning, and what they are designing and building is *competency-based education* (also called competency education).[1] If you have decided to become an architect of the future of your school, or if you are interested in contemporary education, *Competency-Based Education* was written for you.

I became involved with helping schools and school districts develop their competency-based learning systems in New Hampshire in 2007. Because of new state policies enacted in 2005, high school students could only earn credit for a course by showing that they met course competencies. This new requirement opened the opportunity to go beyond the classical Carnegie unit, which is defined by seat time. Learning outside the classroom was now acknowledged and counted as credit if the competencies for the course were met. As I began helping teachers define high-quality competencies and design performance assessments for those competencies, my own thinking in competency education developed. If we are serious about bringing all students to competency so they are ready for college and careers, we must address how and why we structure our schools throughout the K–12 learning experience. In working with many schools in New Hampshire, and nationally over the past ten years, I have seen a new framework for competency education—a blueprint different from that found in traditional schooling—begin to emerge.

This book provides this new blueprint for teachers, principals, and district leaders who seek to become the architects of the future of education for their schools and districts. It offers an overview of competency education and explains how to evolve and redesign your current school structure. Every school embraces this work differently, with different entry points, resources, and structures in place. Creating a one-size-fits-all template for competency education would be no better than rebirthing traditional education. Every school or district that embraces the move toward competency education has a unique civic, cultural, learning, and professional footprint. Charter schools, private and independent schools, and public schools each have their own unique governance and financing structures. In addition to the unique profile of each school that embraces competency education, their motivations for this move may differ.

Contrary to our expectations, competency education can look very different in different schools and communities. As a society, we are used to all schools looking basically the same in all communities across our country. Shifting this paradigm becomes a leadership challenge that requires a long-term commitment to a new vision for learning. It also calls on educators to draw on their own expertise and that of their colleagues to become innovators.

An important question readers must ask themselves as they contemplate competency education is, Why change? Some of you may have evidence that your current model is meeting the needs of *each* of your students to be fully college and career ready on graduation. If so, then your current model is working for you. Others of you may have realized that continual attempts to change the curriculum or otherwise tweak the traditional system have not improved student outcomes. Or you may have found that despite efforts to regroup students for instruction within grade levels, you have persistent cohorts of students unable to demonstrate adequate growth in their learning over time. For you, continually trying to improve the existing system just hasn't worked. You are faced with the reality that if students at the elementary level never really reach their full learning potential during those years, they may never be ready for success later in college or workforce settings. This book is written for you—to guide you as you become the architect of the future of your school.

In *Off the Clock: Moving Education from Time to Competency*, Fred Bramante and I defined competency-based learning as any pace, anyplace, anytime learning. In our book, we explored this concept in detail within the context of New Hampshire's journey to competency education since 2005.[2] We believe passionately that time is the barrier that has shackled education into a traditional mode of teaching and learning—a tradition that can be broken. Shareholders of a learner-centered—not time-centered—vision need to embrace the notion that children learn day in and day out, in school and out of school, in winter and summer, in brick-and-mortar schools and online, and in community settings. We need to create an educational system that supports the reality of learning in today's society. Consequently, the shareholders of competency-based learning systems include the students themselves and all who touch their lives: parents, teachers, school leaders, school policy makers, and community members.

In this new book, I take you deeper into the constructs of competency education and introduce you to a wealth of tools that will support your developmental work in competency education. The competency-based education (CBE) framework introduced in this book is firmly based on the educational research that has led to best practices in K–12 curricula, instruction, assessment, and grading.[3] Using this body of research and the findings from current work in competency education, teachers and leaders can best adapt the new constructs of competency education to the unique teaching and learning cultures of their school. Tools that support this work, as well as a wealth of practical examples of how schools have developed their competency education models, will be featured throughout the book. Drawing from the large network of educators doing this work nationally, the book will introduce the work of CBE pioneers through essays they've written for this volume. In these "Voices from the Field" essays, teachers and other school leaders will share their perspectives and experience on the work that has taken place in their school or district.

Although there are many ways of implementing competency education, this book describes four pillars that make up CBE: competencies (including academic competencies as well as personal success skills such as communication, creativity, collaboration, and self-direction); performance assessment; learning pathways; and competency-based grading. Special attention is paid to the challenges to the development of this work, especially in public schools. Laying a foundation for a new vision of education within a community is difficult but important work. Vision setting and leadership guide the design and implementation to transform teaching and learning to CBE over many years.

Because every learner's journey is unique to the person's particular talents, learning assets, and challenges, we are called to design for the masses systems that can deliver customized, personal learning approaches. A competency education system also recognizes that academic success alone is not the true measure of the learning and proficiency required for students to be ready for, and successful in, the next phase of their lives. But how do we teach and assess those personal success skills as part of the K–12 continuum of learning? This question lies at the heart of student-centered learning. As architects of the future of your school district, you will find that answering this question is an essential part of the design work.

There's an often-repeated saying, "Don't let schooling interfere with your education." With that in mind, I sincerely hope that *Competency-Based Education* helps you overcome the barriers to your work in moving teaching and learning into its future design. We owe this to our learners, our educators, our families, and our communities.

Chapter 1

A New Architecture of Schooling

COMPETENCY EDUCATION IS a fundamental transformation of our education systems. By design, we have historically always expected our students to move efficiently along a learning pathway dictated by a time-based definition of content and skills assigned to discrete grade levels and courses. Grading systems are designed to tell us whether a student knows something on the day of a test, but fail to tell us whether the student can actually put the knowledge to use. Today, we know that this isn't enough to prepare every one of our students for their future paths in life. We must provide the learning environment that enables each child to acquire the knowledge and skills for the student to be ready for higher education and workforce performance expectations. This transformation shifts the focus from the teacher and teaching to the learner and learning. Although our traditional approach to teaching and learning may have served students well in the past, many problems in education today make it difficult to continually improve the existing time-based system. We have essentially been trying to fix the students so that they fit our conventional architecture of grade-level-determined curricula. But the system can no longer be fixed. We should ask ourselves if the time has finally come for us to transform or fundamentally rebuild the system that supports student learning.

If we transform the learning process so that the curriculum would fit the student, rather than the other way around, competency-based education (CBE) could allow for the personalization necessary to meet the needs of every student. CBE introduces a different orientation to the structure and function of our schools. Schools will look and feel different. CBE *is* new the architecture for schools. It is founded as much on a philosophical shift as it is on a shift in the traditional teaching and learning structure in our schools. Let's examine what it means to stretch the thinking from conventional designs of teaching and learning to one where students and their learning sit at the center of all elements in the K–12 journey.

Consider when students aren't performing well in math. Typically, most districts will focus on the curriculum or program that is being used. To remedy the "problem" of low achievement scores, many districts will begin anew to train teachers in a new district-wide math program. All teachers are trained in the same way on how to implement this new math program. Curriculum budget cycles for such adoptions also usually push such initiatives. In asking teachers why they adopted a curriculum, the short answer is always "To improve student test scores." That may be true, but what has been overlooked in the process? Does the one-size-fits-all program meet the individual needs of the students who need to improve those scores? Is there a focus on where the learner is on their developmental continuum for mathematical skills and reasoning? Is every student ready to take the program's test on the same day? We need to rethink this cookie-cutter approach of baking in the same content and curriculum within a defined time and then administering a test to all students at the same time. There is a better way to think about what teaching and learning should look like in our schools. We need to reexamine the structure of our learning environments and mold them to how our students learn.

NEW SYSTEMS FOR LEARNING

Most schools that have pursued CBE have held fast to the five-part definition of competency education developed in 2011 by the International Association for K–12 Online Learning (iNACOL):

- Students advance upon (demonstrated) mastery.
- Competencies include explicit, measurable, transferable learning objectives that empower students.

- Assessment is meaningful and a positive learning experience for students.
- Students receive timely, differentiated support based on their individual learning needs.
- Learning outcomes emphasize competencies that include application and creation of knowledge, along with the development of important skills and dispositions.[1]

Many of the schools highlighted in this book have used this five-part definition to transform their systems. However, in a reflective blog, writer Chris Sturgis suggests that CBE can also be seen as a robust, systemic, *structural* approach for managing a new way to learn:

> Competency education is a system of beliefs and assumptions based on research about child development, learning, and motivation . . .
>
> Competency education is a structure designed to ensure students' needs are being met as well as a structure that enables flexibility in the delivery of educational services . . .
>
> Competency education is a district or school policy that claims responsibility for helping students reach proficiency—not just recall or comprehension, but a level of proficiency that means students can use what they are learning . . .
>
> Mostly importantly, competency education is a method of management.[2]

The detail she provides helps to clarify and address the assumptions we currently hold but rarely question in how we operate our schools. Let's explore the implications of these assumptions to think more deeply about where our current systems will need fundamental rethinking of the design elements.

As federal and state accountability measures ramped up in the early 2000s, the subject area or discipline silos became the breeding ground for coverage of content that bulldozed over much of what we know from research about how students learn.[3] The notion that students learn best by connecting broad concepts was set aside as teachers, faced with tight pacing guides for coverage of content, assessed students for their content knowledge using high-stakes, low-level pencil-and-paper assessment tests given to all students at the same time. This approach to assessment also ignored important educational research showing that the socio-emotional dimensions of learning affect how a student adjusts to school and learns every day.[4] Yet, very little of this information is found in the standards-based curriculum or in assessment practices today. The inflexibly scheduled day, fixed interventionists' schedules, and pacing of the curriculum overrules the need for a student to learn to proficiency in whatever time is needed to do so.[5] Students need time for a sequence of learning that allows them to activate prior knowledge, explore new concepts, acquire new content, practice new skills, and apply this new learning in relevant tasks. They need to do so at their own pace with appropriate support, not at the pace dictated by the curriculum guide. When asked, educators simply say they don't have time for that—districts require fidelity and pacing to fixed curriculum objectives.

We educators therefore face the challenge of flexibly delivering a curriculum that is based on how students individually engage with it and learn it to proficiency. Such an approach simply doesn't fit the cohort- and time-based structure of school today. We have the educational research to guide our decision making, and we need to honor it, even if it means changing school structure as we know it today.

At the heart of this new educational landscape is the concept of bringing each student to competency and the schools' responsibility for doing so. In many classrooms, students simply move on in their grade-level curriculum, even after receiving failing grades. Holding our students responsible for their learning by designing learning opportunities and other sources of support best suited for their needs adds the new dimension of bringing students to competency in their learning to ensure that they are ready for their next new learning experience.

As professionals in an industry—and indeed, education is an industry—we are some of the few who do not demand performance standards. Yes, we do have standards, plenty of them. However, these standards should be the hub for the instructional delivery of content that students then apply to problem-solving or other real-world situations. Such instructional delivery would bring in a set of skills we recognize as important but often fail to teach with intentionality. Critical thinking, problem solving, creativity, collaboration, and self-direction represent what we hope kids learn every day that they come to school. But these skills are often left out of instructional planning. In the era of the No Child Left Behind (NCLB) Act, we just expected that kids would learn what was dictated by the standards—or not—and then move on to the next unit of instruction. However, close inspection of many of the standards reveals that many are not performance standards. So, if you ask students from a traditional high school what they need to do to graduate, they will tell you that they need to pass *x* number of courses. Ask those graduates what they need to do to walk across the stage and receive their diploma, you may be met with a very long pause.

In contrast, robust, clear competencies measured by performance tasks, which are shared with the students in competency-based environments, ensure that students cannot only describe what they are learning, but, also why and how they will use it in a relevant task or exhibition of learning to demonstrate proficiency. Perhaps they will even explain how they will use it five or ten years from now. This is a different graduate! Chapter 2 will describe a community-based process for developing a vision for a community's graduates. This foundational activity enables all stakeholders to understand how CBE can ensure that their graduates are college and career ready when that diploma passes into the graduates' hand.

The NCLB era has generated great warehouses of student data to document which students meet the standards and which students do not. Great effort and resources are then expended on pushing more of the low-achieving students to at least meet the proficiency cut score for the test. At the same time, public education often doesn't spend enough time honoring the students who consistently are proficient. We often can do no better than hold them to a curriculum they already know, because we can't figure out how to flexibly group students beyond a single classroom for instructional purposes to challenge proficient learners with a curriculum more suited to where they are in their learning. For example, student data can show that a student in grade 4 may have a sixth-grade reading ability, but the student will be given reading materials consistently at the fourth-grade level because that is what is dictated by grade-level curriculum. Herein lies the heart of the future of education—redefining and redesigning our systems to make sure that all students move forward, learning at their own pace and with the support they need to meet proficiency on defined competencies.

Central to the understanding of CBE is the definition of competency: Competency is the ability of a student to *apply* or *transfer* content and skills in or across content areas. In understanding the significance of this statement, we turn from the low-level expectations of teacher-centric coverage of the curriculum (i.e., the drill, fill, and kill approach) to looking for evidence of student learning through performance criteria. The ability of students to apply content and skills to use strategic or extended thinking in the learning opportunity is at the heart of competency. An analogy might be a physician assistant who, in training, may do very well in content courses such as physiology, anatomy, pharmacology, and biochemistry. If the individual can't convert this learning into an ability to problem-solve in the diagnosis of a patient, he or she may not pass the professional phase of training or national boards. In traditional education, we have been "filling our students up" with content in the hopes that they will know what to do with it when it is time to apply it later. CBE requires that we build ecosystems of learning to bring students to competencies, however long it takes and wherever it needs to happen. This approach also means that students must demonstrate proficiency by applying their learning before they move on to new learning.

> **COMPETENCY** is the ability of a student to *apply* or *transfer* content and skills in or across content areas.

As we design and shift to CBE, we essentially will be moving our kids to a phase of learning analogous to how the physician assistant learns to diagnose a patient. In short, our students must demonstrate proficiency on performance standards or competencies for their graduation. The design of graduation competencies, performance assessments, versatile learning pathways, and dynamic (competency-based) grading systems that include critical twenty-first-century skills, which I call personal success skills, are the architectural support of competency education.

THE SHIFTS

Competency education isn't simply about adding elements onto our traditional system of teaching and learning. It is a fundamental systemic shift. Figure 1.1

FIGURE 1.1   The shifts from traditional education to competency-based education

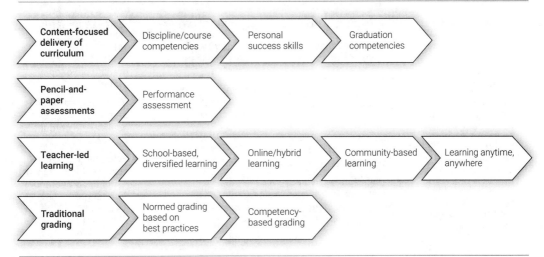

lays out these shifts. In competency education, the four pillars of traditional education—content-focused curriculum, pencil-and-paper assessments, teacher-led learning, and grades expressed as an average of all learning (including assorted other nonacademic factors)—are replaced with well-defined graduation competencies; performance assessments; the option for anytime, anywhere learning; and competency grading that reports progress toward twenty-first-century skills separately from the ability to apply knowledge. Educators contemplating moving toward CBE need to recognize that, given their local culture for teaching and learning, some of these shifts may be very difficult. By describing these shifts to the CBE framework, this book will help educators make the shifts more purposefully and successfully.

THE COMPETENCY-BASED EDUCATION FRAMEWORK FOR LEARNING

A core belief about learning is that students come in with their own assets, learning preferences, and developmental needs. Our teacher-centric model of curriculum design, batched testing, whole-class instruction, and questionable, subjective grading practices may not meet the needs of all students. As table 1.1 illustrates, the CBE framework provides the architecture to transform current traditional school

TABLE 1.1   The architecture of competency-based education

(handwritten margin notes: "Master Competencies")

COMPETENCIES	PERFORMANCE ASSESSMENTS	LEARNING PATHWAYS	COMPETENCY-BASED GRADING
▪ K–12 district competencies for all academic disciplines informed by standards ▪ Grade-level and course competencies aligned to K–12 competencies ▪ Learning progressions that support competency development ▪ K–12 personal success skills defined and incorporated into a personal learning plan	▪ Performance tasks for assessing competence ▪ Rubrics to assess tasks ▪ Performance indicators to assess readiness ▪ Formative assessment triggers relearning, summative assessment when student is ready ▪ Multiple and varied assessments inform evaluation of Competent	▪ Guided by a K–12 personal learning plan ▪ Systemic resources to support personalization ▪ Project-based learning ▪ Blended and online learning ▪ Extended learning opportunities (ELOs) ▪ Opportunities for choice, voice, and student agency in deeper learning	▪ Teacher practice guided by K–12 grading philosophy statements ▪ "Rolling" grades reflect progress toward unit, course, and graduation competencies ▪ Relearning and reassessment to bring students to competency without grade penalties

designs into a learner-centric system through the implementation of four pillars: competencies, performance assessments, learning pathways, and competency-based grading.

Competencies

In the CBE framework, competencies need to be thought of first as graduation competencies, or K–12 competencies. What competencies must students show evidence of mastery to walk across that stage for the handshake at the end of the journey? In light of these competencies, what needs to be learned and demonstrated along the way? In chapter 3, we will examine how these competencies are designed and how several schools have built competencies for academics and personal success skills into their existing K–12 curriculum designs.

Academic competencies are demonstrated through the application of content and skills defined by the learning progressions identified by a school district. Imagine lifting the essential standards out of grade levels and creating a continuous progression of content and skills. This progression should be built from kindergarten through twelfth grade, in a coherent learning continuum of increasing complexity in every academic area. In the CBE framework, this academic progression is only one piece of the learning progression leading to graduation. Additionally shaping the progression toward competency are all the other influences in learning—social-emotional, physical, psychological, academic orientation, and individual interests as well as so-called soft skills, or dispositions.

In chapter 3, we will examine how to create high-quality, coherent academic competencies that define the learning continuum from kindergarten to twelfth grade. Today, much of our curriculum is isolated by levels: K–6, 7–8, and so forth, and by courses within disciplines at the high school. Developing K–12 academic competencies focuses on the learning progressions across all the levels leading to the expected learning outcomes that a graduate from high school should know and can do. Many schools and districts use Understanding by Design (UbD), a reverse-engineering educational planning tool developed by Grant Wiggins and Jay McTighe, as their approach to unit-based teaching. In this book, the UbD model is adapted to the design of competency-based units of instruction to help guide teachers move their current work into the CBE framework.

Personal Success Skills

Academics alone do not prepare our youth for college or career readiness. Although very few would argue with the preceding observation, education has not directly addressed the importance of nonacademic learning as part of schools' teaching or assessment practices. Recently, educators have begun to address these soft skills, sometimes called noncognitive skills, nonacademic skills, or dispositions. Chapter 4 will discuss the most recent research on the skills that should be both taught and assessed in learning activities. For the purposes of the CBE framework, I call these skills *personal success skills* because parents and members of the business community readily recognize these skills as important for mature, independent graduates from high school.

Performance Assessments

Competency education implies learning by doing, followed by showing that you know. As we will see in chapter 5, if competency requires a demonstration of learning, the demonstration must be assessed through performance. Rich performance tasks require higher-order thinking to apply learned content and skill.

Complex tasks designed to measure multiple competencies provide a rich learning and assessment environment. In any profession, competency is never demonstrated by a single performance on one day. Competency is developed over time. As learning tasks and assessments of these tasks are developed and mapped along the learning continuum, students get various opportunities to demonstrate competency. The criteria for competency become more complex along the journey. For example, the competency criteria built in to writing a piece in argumentation for a sixth-grade student may not have the same level of complexity as that expected of a student who is about to graduate from high school. By defining these expectations clearly along the way, students show evidence of their college and career readiness in many ways and at different times.

It is often difficult to break away from thinking that a paper-and-pencil test must be used to grade learning. These types of tests become only one of many types of assessments in the CBE classroom because they often can't capture performance very well. As students learn new content and practice new skills, their learning—and its assessment—is considered formative. During this time, both the student and the teacher play an important role in determining student readiness to move on to applying their learning in more complex tasks. These tasks are summative demonstrations of proficiency. The biggest shift in thinking about assessment between the traditional, batch-test approach and that used in CBE is how and when students are assessed.

Traditionally, paper-and-pencil summative assessments administered at the end of a unit of work are given to all students at the same time, despite earlier evidence that a student has not learned the underlying content and skills. Often, the questions on such tests are of questionable quality (e.g., 250 questions on a Scantron form), testing only a student's retention of content for the purposes of the test. A pencil-and-paper test has narrowly defined summative assessment. In reality, such a test may be one of many types of summative assessments. It is really just a format for an assessment.

In a competency-based environment, a summative assessment is never invoked unless there is evidence from assessments of the formative learning that a student is ready for it. Such formative evidence may indicate that a student is having difficulty with the underlying content and skills and is clearly not ready for its application. In this case, relearning must take place at the time of this formative work. Teachers understand that a student cannot move on until he or she has grasped the underlying concepts. But coming from the traditional mind-set, they are unsure how to address this quandary in everyday practice. Chapter 5 will show the complexity of performance tasks by examining their design as well as the design of project-based learning, extended learning opportunities, and capstone experiences.

All assessment processes use tools to score student proficiency. These tools are rubrics to score the products of student learning in performance tasks. Chapter 5 shows how to build good rubrics whose achievement-level descriptors can form the foundation of competency-based grading systems.

Educators design inquiry-based performance tasks to give students the opportunity to learn deeply. Through engaging scenarios that students may even cocreate, students can take the point of inquiry into research and then create a product or presentation, or both. Because such tasks are mapped against competencies and entered into grade books by competency, the assessors are able to evaluate, over time, a student's proficiency in any competency.

Learning Pathways

Learning pathways are the journeys that learners take in their education. Chapter 6 describes how important these pathways are to the anytime, anywhere, learning in which students are empowered by opportunities to choose what and how they learn. The pathways are documented in a K–12 personal learning plan and lead to graduation and a high school diploma. The traditional learning pathway is based on the assumption that only what students learn through the approved K–12 curriculum is valuable. It is also based almost entirely on learning that takes place in a face-to-face encounter with teachers in brick-and-mortar schools. But our students are learning all the time. There are rich sources outside for learning for our students: technology-based learning opportunities, either formal through online learning or the informal learning out of curiosity; summer camp experiences; community-based educational programs; and opportunities in the arts and sciences at museums or other institutions. Yet we only take measure of learning in our classrooms. Many of our students' lives are shaped by experiences outside the classroom, yet we seldom respect or even take advantage of what students learn in these experiences.

The purpose of a personal learning plan is to tap into a student's assets, personal and academic goals, aspirations, learning preferences, and personal reflection of all their learning along the way, regardless of where it takes place. This all-inclusiveness is at the heart of personalization. The learner and his or her learning team of parents and educators cocreate the learning opportunities and incorporate this 24/7/365 learning in making decisions. The choice and voice that a student develops over time enriches the learning progression toward graduation and makes the learning progress a very personal experience.

In hearing about the importance of outside experiences in learning, some teachers are a bit threatened at first because they feel it diminishes their role. But when I point out how rich this information is in making their work with students much more meaningful, they see the sense of it all. Personalization of this nature can be overwhelming for a teacher to think about if the frame of reference comes from one teacher having numerous classes. Technology-enabled learning can unleash powerful opportunities for personalization and facilitates the teacher responsibilities of managing learning opportunities.

Competency-Based Grading

In developing a student learning pathway leading toward graduation, we need to communicate the growing expertise a student develops across the many learning opportunities on his or her pathway. In working with many school districts to move toward competency-based grading systems, I have found that grading can be the most difficult part of constructing their CBE system.

In chapter 7, I outline the best course of reforming traditional grading to competency-based grading and provide examples of how this shift can best be done as part of comprehensive CBE. The shift in the culture of teaching and learning must precede any major grading system changes. As the language and culture for learning changes, grading practices can also change. The development of a K–12 grading philosophy statement or comprehensive grading policy normalizes good teacher grading practices across all grade levels and effectively extinguishes bad grading practices inherent in the traditional framework. Fair and responsible grading also provides both validity and reliability in the student grades, minimizing the subjective grading found in traditional grading systems. Competency-based grading not based on averages, but is based on rolling grades that reflect progress toward unit, course, and graduation competencies, and it offers opportunities to relearn and reassess to bring students to competency without penalties along the way. Chapter 7 will also delve into the use of software to help teachers with learning, assessment, and personalization.

LEADERSHIP

The transformation of schools and districts to CBE requires strong leadership. In ten years of coaching school leaders through this process, I have seen several qualities emerge from school leaders engaged in this transformation. I discuss these qualities in chapter 8. Recently, CompetencyWorks, an online resource promoting CBE, examined several New England states to determine why they were making such headway toward competency education at the state and local levels. One key finding was leadership. Transforming districts takes strong leadership at both the district and the local levels. The district can't transform without an enabling policy environment with a suite of support for the local entities. Also, to support educators in this transformation, schools and districts must develop and enforce pro-transformation school policies.[6] Chapter 8 will showcase the leadership skills that many of the school leaders—both administrators and teachers—exhibit as they have undertaken the innovative work of transforming their schools and districts.

CASE STUDIES

Because competency education has only been at the forefront of new designs and approaches in education relatively recently, it is difficult to find a school or district that has completely moved from a traditional to a competency-based system. Most schools and districts are in the process of this transformation, and they generally start the work at a place of their own choosing. Chapter 9 will look closely at two public school districts that have been making the transformation for many years, yet are still evolving their models. For the past twenty years, the Chugach School District in Alaska has worked tirelessly to structure its schools to best support the culture and learning of the students in a community-based approach. The remarkable story allows us to understand the many decisions the district reached along the way. While Chugach is a very rural school district, the Sanborn Regional School District, a larger district in southeastern New Hampshire, has its own story of moving to CBE. These two case studies are not the only models of school redesign in CBE, but because of the unique nature of the challenges facing public education, the Chugach and Sanborn stories should inspire public educators to undertake this work on behalf of their students.

NEW DESIGNS, NEW ACCOUNTABILITY

As new models in competency education emerged in public education in New Hampshire since 2005, it became apparent that NCLB high-stakes, state-level accountability testing was inadequate in determining student proficiency. Chapter 10 recounts New Hampshire's journey to build a new accountability system—incorporating common performance tasks at most grades in place of high-stakes tests—and the challenges of bringing the new system to scale statewide. The New Hampshire Performance Assessment for Competency Education (NH PACE) pilot is built on the premise that a test on one day cannot adequately determine a student's proficiency. The theory of action in this pilot was to develop a system of accountability based on multiple measures of student performance while supporting both teachers and students in the process. New Hampshire's PACE pilot will inform other innovations in state assessment programs under the 2015 federal legislation, the Every Student Succeeds Act (ESSA).

As you consider all aspects of CBE, you may see ways to shift your thinking away from the traditional mind-set that has hampered schools for generations. This book can help you make these shifts, to uncover the exciting possibilities that a school can offer its students as they get ready to enter the greater world around them.

Chapter 2

Envisioning a New Graduate

WHAT WILL GRADUATES of your high school need to be successful as they embark on the next chapter of their lives—either in higher education or the workforce? Or, in essence, what should it take for your graduates to walk across the stage having truly earned the diploma and congratulatory handshake at graduation? This question is critical in laying the foundation for teaching and learning across the K–12 continuum. This is also a question that I often use to begin my work assisting school leaders who are hoping to adopt CBE and recommend it to others. Seeking the answer to this question by drawing on input from parent, students, and community members is often the first step in designing the future of a school or district.

Remarkably, most of the kids in our schools today were born in this century while education still tries to reckon with moving "toward" the twenty-first century. The kids are already ahead of us before they step into our schools! We need to pause, think through where we are in education today, and hit the reset button on the current structure and function of our schools. A reset means that we need to take inventory of what we currently are doing, why are we doing it, what we need to do to prepare our students for their future, and how are we going to do it. We need to accept that the "it" needs to look different from the "it" of generations past.

b 1980 - 1997

Today, the millennial generation, defined as those who were eighteen to thirty-four years old in 2015, surpasses the number of baby boomers in our population.[1] Quite a bit of attention has been given to how millennials are reshaping today's workplace and how, as a generation, these "digital natives" pose a challenge for many in older generations. Although all but the very youngest of the millennial generation have already grown through our K–12 school systems, it was only during the past ten years that we have become more aware of how different millennials are as learners. This difference has created tension in our schools, especially around technology integration in the learning process and an ever-growing need for education to be personalized.

As school and community leaders set a vision for learning, they must recognize that many of the parents of our current students are millennials who have different expectations for their children. Are you surprised to know that 43 percent of children from birth to seventeen years old had millennial parents in 2014 and that 85 percent of all babies born in 2013 had millennial moms?[2] Those babies of 2013 are already in our preschools and will be the kindergarten class of 2018.

Researchers have found that millennials, as parents, demand greater convenience as they avail themselves of tech-enabled innovation in their everyday work and home life.[3] They embrace digitization in their daily tasks, from how they travel (e.g., Uber and Lyft) to the wearable technology they buy.

For good or bad, millennials expect instant gratification. In so demanding this, they have shaped the demand for some of the modern conveniences we all appreciate, such as free shipping for online orders and the sharing of day-to-day life, decisions, pastimes, and entertainment via social media. As consumers, millennials have had their spending habits tracked closely. They tend to reject mass-produced items for more customized or specialized items for their children. As school leaders, we should recognize these attributes and use them to shape the education that millennial parents want for their children. When they exert their influence on the education systems they want for the future, millennial parents may very well be as disruptive to education as they have been in other areas of our culture.

Educational leaders should capitalize on these generational tendencies and encourage millennial parents to participate in, and be accepting of, different ways of educating the new generation. Neil Howe, a nationally renowned author and expert in generational studies, who has extensively researched generational tendencies, has also identified characteristics of this new generation (which he calls the *homeland generation*) of special interest to education.[4] The homeland generation—the offspring of the millennial generation—is the most diverse generation in history. Its members are the products of declining birth and fertility rates and are born to parents older than were earlier generations of parents. This group is shaped by extremely protective parents. Ask teachers in our classrooms today, and they generally agree that protectiveness is at play every day. Most striking, Howe's latest research found that parents of this new generation push for academic achievement in ways not seen in the earlier generations. These parents want their children in preschool at earlier and earlier ages. Along with this new emphasis on academic achievement, millennial parents have a renewed focus on social development. As you begin thinking through the design elements of the CBE framework, you will see that its elements are very responsive to this new generation of parents and students before us.

As school leaders, we often expect that any conversation around school reform will be difficult. However, if we ask the right questions and engage parents and other community members to elicit their opinions before we discuss any transformation, moving forward in school reform may be easier than we think. When parents and other community members are involved from the beginning, they will help carry the message that we need to restructure our institutions to be responsive to the generation of students in front of us every day. Their yearning for personalization and customization, their use of technology as part of daily life, their protective nature, and their emphasis on social development and academic achievement should help us to transform our schools.

Engaging the community in setting a vision is a way to uncover everyone's thinking about their hopes and aspirations for their children. If this foundational work with parents and community members is done well, it will give educational leaders a natural opportunity to lay the groundwork for introducing CBE as a system for providing the type of learning environment that fits with the demands of parents today. This process is far different from the annual goal-setting effort and strategic improvement plans we've all been a part of in education. Annual goals and strategic improvement plans serve to improve the existing system. When we begin to develop a community vision for CBE, the goal is to discover what the community values (academically, socially, developmentally, etc.) in their graduates and then design and build the system to produce it.

SETTING THE STAGE FOR LOCAL TRANSFORMATION

As the district outreach competency education specialist for the New Hampshire Department of Education, I have had many opportunities to speak with district staff across the state. In one district, I asked the teachers a similar question to the one that began this chapter: What should their kids be able to do, to be prepared for their future? One teacher pulled me aside and asked if I had seen their mission statement painted on the wall outside the gymnasium. I went out, jotted down the mission statement, and reengaged the staff around the talking points of the statement: "[The school] strives to produce graduates who are academically and socially prepared to be responsible, caring and contributing members of the global society." I asked them, what is the evidence that teaching and learning for each of the elements of their mission statement are actively happening? How does their report card communicate to students and parents that the students are socially responsible and "caring and contributing members of the global society?" What does it mean to be a member of a global society?

The groups then began to discuss the hard and soft skills that kids needed to achieve this vision. There were some important conversations going on in the room. The biggest aha moment came when the teachers realized that their current report card communicated academic achievement only. All the qualities that they believed were the most important in preparing students for success in life never made it onto the report card, because these qualities were not intentionally taught or assessed. When I lead this same activity with parents and other audiences, they too begin to recognize the need to refashion or remodel how we prepare children for higher education and the world of work. Most importantly, they want to engage with the school in growing toward a new vision. Enter competency education.

In the summer of 2015, the Fall Mountain Regional School District began to work on its vision. Fall Mountain, a very rural district in the western part of New Hampshire, is made up of several attendance districts having small rural elementary schools feeding into a small middle and high school. Lori Landry, the visionary superintendent, saw the value and need for the communities to come together to set a common vision and pathway to the future. She had led the district through several strategic plans involving school improvement and believed the district needed to refocus its work. She and others were interested in becoming one of New Hampshire's PACE districts. Setting a common vision, Landry thought, would give a vision and purpose for the work—a vision that could be communicated effectively throughout the district. I was assisting Laundry and her group in developing such a vision. We thought it was important to bring together a balanced cross-section of the various communities to base this new direction on their vision of the future for the school district. With that vision, the district could further develop its curriculum, assessment, learning, grading, and accountability systems. Approximately thirty people gathered for the session, with representation from parents, teachers, administrators, the school board, and the local governments from all the towns in the district.

In preparing the participants for the activity, I drew on the researched-based talking points put forth by the FrameWorks Institute when I spoke to the public on school reform.[5] (See the sidebar "Helping Educators Frame Challenges for the Public.") It wasn't yet the time or the place to design a strategic plan for the future. However, it was the opportunity to hone in on what the community members valued for their children's future. We were interested in opening their thinking about remodeling and refashioning the system toward their future aspirations for their children.

HELPING EDUCATORS FRAME CHALLENGES FOR THE PUBLIC

In a research study conducted by the FrameWorks Institute, a nonprofit organization dedicated to improve public discourse on social problems by presenting scholarly research on a variety of critical topics, two simplifying models emerged as the most effective in engaging the public in issues of school reform.[6] The first model compares school reform to an orchestra. The orchestra comprises many parts that must work together to produce harmony. In seeing school reform through this lens, imagine all the players being given a new piece of music. They would have to work together to make it sound great. Parents and community members, when they understand this analogy, see their role more clearly in the reform project ahead.

The other school-reform model that effectively engages the community is that of remodeling a house. This analogy goes beyond the notion that school reform is fixing a problem. By thinking about remodeling, parents and community members can speak to their own experiences in remodeling and why they remodeled their homes or businesses. It is a meaningful segue to then think through the need for remodeling education. Remodeling goes beyond surface changes. It is future minded, and it is hard work.

The FrameWorks Institute is a rich resource to develop your talking points and approaches when you are speaking with the public. Several resources on this topic can be found at www.frameworksinstitute.org/K-12-education.html.

At the outset of this work, we created a carefully planned list of invitees to ensure representation of the community and a balance of personalities and voices rather than starting with an open invitation. Parent groups were asked to invite parent representatives, school administrators were asked to invite teachers, and so on. We were careful to structure the discussion groups so that they were mixed and changed up for each of the activities. To that end, I designed the "Who Is Your Graduate?" activity, which was focused on the following question:

WHO IS YOUR GRADUATE?

What will the graduates of your high school need to be successful in the next chapter of their lives—either in higher education or in the workforce? In essence, what should it take for your graduate to walk across the stage and earn the handshake at graduation?

I divided the attendees into four groups. Each group was composed of a mixed representation of teachers, parents, administrators, and community members. I ensured the mix simply by number-coding the name tags. The first task for each design group was to brainstorm a list of qualities, abilities (competencies), and other characteristics that they believed a graduate would need to be prepared for the next phase of life in the workforce or higher education. The participants wrote down their thoughts on poster paper set up on easels.

The groups were allowed to discuss this issue at length. When they were finished brainstorming, they posted their posters at different points in the room. They were then all asked to circulate to each of the posters in groups of two or three and circle the items that were compelling to them.

Each group then reclaimed its poster with the circled items. The participants were then asked, as a group, to arrive at a consensus on the circled items on their own poster.

We next captured the thinking of each group and categorized it. The items in bold in the list below represent consensus of the item by several groups or all of them:

> *Academic proficiency*: problem-solving skills, literacy and listening skills, critical thinking skills, ability to apply knowledge
> *Personal (self)*: self-direction, self-reflection or self-awareness, ethics and drive, perseverance, collaboration, integrity and honesty, responsibility, empathy
> *Global and community*: social responsibility, leadership skills, twenty-first-century technology ability and responsibility, historical perspective
> *Other*: Budgeting and checkbook skills, time management skills, reliability, effective communication skills, compassion, passion, continual lifelong learner, happiness

Having identified the areas of consensus and of value to each group, the participants then set about writing a statement that summarized their thoughts. When they finished, we had four vision statements. The statements were then posted and visited by everyone in groups of two or three. This time, they underlined the words that were compelling to them on each of the statements.

At the end of that round, one volunteer from each group was then given the task of moving to a separate room to write a consensus vision statement. Here is what they wrote:

> Upon graduation, Fall Mountain students will have the academic and social abilities to actively apply their knowledge and skills as ethically responsible citizens well-equipped to succeed in their community, country and world.

This activity was meant to immerse the community in thinking differently about a vision for the future. In addition, we wanted to take advantage of the short time—three hours—to tap the community members for their thoughts on the most important drivers to deliver this vision of the future.

To do that, we asked each group to list no more than four drivers that would bring this vision to reality. They needed to think coherently and systemically. Once they identified their four drivers, they posted them on another sheet of poster paper.

Each participant was then given three colored dots, which could be used to mark the three items the participant felt were the most important across the four charts of identified drivers. We needed to pause here because the groups identified some items that only had shades of difference in meaning. We consequently cleaned up some language and crossed-linked similar items. We did this as a group activity and agreed on the three drivers: (1) personalized learning and active engagement; (2) mastery of rigorous academic and social curriculum; and (3) perseverance to achieve.

Note that the working groups didn't identify competency education per se. Later, however, the superintendent introduced competency education as a way to deliver on their vision. The district is currently developing components of the CBE framework. Kristen Wilson, Fall Mountain's curriculum, instruction, and assessment director, is leading the K–12 development of the district's academic competencies and spearheading the development of competency-based performance assessment. The district is also beginning work on its new K–12 grading system. Wilson describes the work in "Voices from the Field: The Importance of Vision."

VOICES FROM THE FIELD

THE IMPORTANCE OF VISION

By Kristin M. Wilson, MEd, CAGS, Director of Curriculum, Instruction, and Assessment at Fall Mountain Regional School District

Many, if not all, schools or districts have taken the time to write a mission statement. Fall Mountain is no different in that respect. Our purpose for existing is presented through our mission statement and describes the *now* of our work and focuses on what we will accomplish with our students. Where we differ from most districts is in looking ahead and defining our vision of the graduate, or our vision for the future—the *why* of our work. We gathered teachers, school board members, parents, local business leaders, staff members, administrators, and other community members together to help us in determining the skills our students would have by graduation and what they would be able to do with those skills. Our discussions moved from talking about the what to the why and shifted from the result to the journey with students.

Superintendent Lori Landry and I have also been taking the vision-of-the-graduate activity around to each of the schools and doing some generative thinking with them. It has been amazing to hear the staff's thoughts. We're spreading a message to teachers about engaging in innovative thinking and being willing to take risks with lessons and assessments. The superintendent and I have discussed modeling both innovative thinking and risk-taking (and more) for our students. We've also built on the future protocol we completed with the administrative team and a group of staff that attended the Sanborn Design Institute last summer. (In response to the popular demand for educators to visit the Sanborn Regional School District, the district chose to provide a design opportunity for teams of teachers and leaders from districts across the country to learn how Sanborn transformed its district. The Sanborn Design Institute provides the learning opportunity and the design time and space in the summer for teachers and other leaders to consult local Sanborn teachers and leaders in CBE and begin their district's CBE design process.) Landry and I went around the district and completed the future protocol with each school as well as with the community one evening. We're compiling the information now, and the administrative team is going to use it to plan our next steps.

> The vision work we have completed so far has created a transformation in our school district. We use the vision of the graduate to align our district and school goals, determine and plan our professional learning, ground our discussions, and help drive our decisions. It has become a driving force within our district.

TAKING THE NECESSARY TIME

As is the case for any worthwhile venture that requires a significant change in the mind-set of great numbers of stake holders, the creation of a new vision for a school district takes time. For example, in another group of New Hampshire school districts, the leaders chose to spend an entire school year to work with their communities in developing their vision for the future. This school administrative unit (SAU) is made up of six school districts, each of them having its own school board for governance. In setting a vision with all the representative shareholders across each of the districts, the leaders believed it was important to take enough time. The SAU has been challenged by several constituencies with the question "Why change?" The SAU represents small towns with high incomes and high performing students. Because New Hampshire requires all its school districts to have district competencies in place by July 2017, the leadership of the SAU started with an inclusive process to ask, "Who is our graduate?" After collecting the feedback from approximately twenty audiences, the leaders fashioned a vision for the multitown SAU. Throughout the school year that the vision work was carried out locally, two teams of educators met to build their understanding of the CBE framework. One group of K–5 educators and a group of grade 6–12 educators worked monthly to learn about CBE and to study various models. In the summer that followed, the two teams then worked more intensively on their CBE framework. The SAU office created a CBE website to provide a common professional resource for all the work.

In a summer institute, the teachers gathered all the input obtained from the public meetings and consolidated it into one statement. In exploring the vision statement, we carried out a future protocol for the participants to project their vision into the future. What would this vision look like for both students and teachers? To further personalize the process, we created personae—typical students at each level and teachers at various experience levels. We drew pictures of these personae, described their characteristics, and did an exercise that put the personae through the vision of the future the participants had created earlier. Sometimes, adults tend to plan for solutions that best meet adult needs. But by using student personae, the participants discussed how different students would learn as the district's vision was realized. It smoothly shifted the thinking from adult needs to student needs. By imagining how both children and adults in the system would experience the new CBE approach, the teachers could more realistically plan for the future transformation.

The next stage of work was the initial planning stage. It was not intended to be a highly structured multiyear plan. Having identified what the future would look like, the group next needed to define the boosts and barriers to the vision of the future. *Boosts* are the elements currently in place that would promote the vision. *Barriers* are features that may impede or present other problems in promoting the vision.

Defining the boosts and barriers has proven very helpful for groups to gain consensus on the good work currently going on in the district. The exercise also helps the groups agree on the real barriers that may threaten productive planning and implementation of the work.

For many districts, the boosts commonly include positive school culture; a professional development program viewed as meaningful and important by teachers; strong professional learning communities empowered to use innovative strategies in teaching; active and involved parent organizations; and communities that financially support education.

The barrier most often cited in this exercise is time. Teachers generally feel that there is not enough professional time and not enough resources to create the systems that support their vision. In several instances, the constraints found in the collective bargaining agreement were seen as a barrier to developmental work. For instance, in one district, the principal had no leeway in changing the after-school schedule of teacher meetings, because of contractual issues. Another commonly identified barrier is access to technology that supports personalized learning. Whatever barriers are identified, it is important to face them directly and decide at the outset whether the barrier is insurmountable or whether there is a way to work around it. Detours such as these are not welcome but are sometimes necessary to the long-term success in a school transformation plan.

BLUEPRINT FOR A VISION

In the middle of many traditional school improvement projects, teachers sometimes ask, "Why are we doing this, anyway?" This sense on the teachers' part that a project seems irrelevant exemplifies the difference between school improvement and school transformation. By comprehensively resetting the educational vision, competency education becomes the vehicle to carry students, staff, parents, and the community into the future. The why of this work is compelling and always at the forefront of the designers' minds.

As you develop your blueprint for the future, I encourage you to take the time necessary to comprehensively determine your community's vision of its graduate. Don't just ask high school parents. Ask your elementary school parents. They have the greatest stake in supporting their vison of the graduate. As you develop this vision, explore what they think the journey toward the future will look like for students and teachers. Be realistic about which current assets or boosts will catapult your work forward, but also be honest about the very real barriers to this work.

With such a community-based vision, educators can create the pathways that prepare the graduate for their handshake at graduation. The added bonus will be new relationships with your parents, staff, and community.

Chapter 3

Competencies

WHICH COMPETENCIES SIGNAL that a student is graduation ready? How can we provide evidence that the student has demonstrated the required proficiency along the learning continuum leading up to graduation—evidence that assures students (and parents) that graduation from high school means they will be ready for college or the workplace? If we aren't ready to measure success or proficiency along the way, our students will fall into the same learning gaps they fell into in traditional education. For this reason, we need to design a system of competencies that grow across the K–12 curriculum. In setting a vision, community members consistently recognize that academic skills are not the only hallmarks of success. Thus, in our CBE framework, we recognize the need to create this continuum of academic competencies along with the other qualities we recognize as important to success in later life—personal success skills. These competencies are developmentally based and embedded within the learning continuum leading to graduation. Academic competencies, expressed as competency statements and based on essential standards within content areas, together with an articulation of desired personal success skills, build a learning progression over time. In the CBE framework, this learning progression can take place in a variety of settings, from face-to-face brick-and-mortar schools to online or community settings.

Several months ago, I was waiting outside a treatment room of a local hospital while my husband was undergoing an echocardiogram. I was ushered out of the room when the technician told me she had to do an extra procedure because of what she had seen on the test. Standing outside the room, I looked at the wall, only to find this: "The American Registry for Diagnostic Medical Sonographers hereby certifies that [technician's name], Registered Diagnostic Cardiac Sonographer, has demonstrated a high level of competency in theory and practice by successfully completing the ARDMS certifying examinations, with a specialty or specialties in Adult Echocardiography." I hadn't known the technician before then, and I have no idea who tested her or what grade she received on her examinations. But I do know that the certificate assured me of her competence to problem-solve the issue my husband had while undergoing this test. The technician had met the standard criteria for performance, demonstrated to a level of proficiency, before that certification was given. In short, in the medical profession, proficiency (competency) must be demonstrated before a person receives the license to independently practice. In many aspects of our lives, we depend on the competence of others to fix our cars, correctly prepare our taxes, give us legal advice, safely drive the eighteen-wheeler rolling down the road next to us, and fill cavities in our teeth. Often, these diplomas or certificates give us the confidence that performance criteria have been met.

Our colleges and businesses have no way to tell from current school transcripts if students have met performance criteria for graduation. In addition, the course content from one high school to another can vary greatly, and the lack of performance criteria in granting credit for courses has eroded the value and meaning of the high school diploma. These shortcomings create great disparity from student to student, high school to high school, community to community, and state to state as students step up for college admission or workplace opportunities. Like the credentials in other industries, high school diplomas should mean that performance criteria for graduation are identified and that the prospective graduate has provided performance evidence of the required knowledge and skills.

Schools need to rethink the notion that credit accrual alone translates into competence and college and career readiness. As in many other industries, it shouldn't matter which institution grants the diploma if the performance criteria for the diploma are the same or comparable. For a high school diploma, we must insist that each high school provide the learning opportunities and performance criteria that provide evidence that the student has met the requirements for college and career readiness. In an ideal world, the performance criteria for a high school diploma would be nationally recognized as the same set of criteria for each granting institution. However, the political and institutional complexity of accomplishing this task may be overwhelming. It shouldn't discourage us from working at the local level, however, and sharing the work within our profession. Building high-quality competencies in K–12 education with performance criteria that are publicly known will begin to address the problem of questionable college and career readiness based solely on credit accrual at the time of graduation. Let's begin there.

The problem we see now is that a time-based curriculum, paced to a school year in a cohort model, results in some learners knowing some of the material some of the time, with test criteria that often fall short of determining true proficiency. Our challenge is to design a continuum of performance-based criteria leading to graduation whereby every student demonstrates his or her proficiency before moving to the next level of that competency. To do this, let's hone in on what is needed to build the pillar of competency within the CBE framework:

- ▸ K–12 district competencies for all academic disciplines informed *"Master"* by standards
- ▸ grade-level and course competencies aligned to K–12 competencies
- ▸ learning progressions that support competency development
- ▸ K–12 personal success skills defined and incorporated into a personal learning plan

COMPETENCY DESIGN IN THE CBE FRAMEWORK

To better understand competency design, we'll consider the design of academic competencies separately from the design of personal success skills. Education has defined disciplinary content areas with sets of content and skills standards. These standards are part of the foundation of good competencies. We will consider how to use these standards to design good competency statements that incorporate how these standards are applied or transferred. By their very nature, personal success skills, the other piece of college and career readiness, are developmental rather than standards based. We will consider their design separately in chapter 4.

Articulated Competencies Across the K–12 Continuum

Designing competencies in every content area across the K–12 continuum may seem daunting, but most school districts have the foundational pieces already in place. If your district has a well-defined K–12 standards-based curriculum for all content areas, your work in designing academic competency statements will be simplified. You can begin with model competency statements already developed by other school, districts, or states. Or you may instead decide to create your own overarching competency statements derived from your existing standards. The most important work will be for teachers to recognize the difference between a standard and a competency.

In working with educators designing these systems, I caution them not to slip into the habit of simply renaming what they currently do. Because you may have a standards-based curriculum, it does not mean you have a competency-based curriculum. Standards define the content and skills of a discipline; they are a necessary part of education. However, many standards do not rise to the level of a competency. It is better to think of a competency as a student's ability to apply *clusters* of standards to execute a particular performance task.

Think of a competency as a student's concept. It is comparable to an enduring understanding or a generalization.[1] To move from your current standards-based curriculum, consider your anchor standards—the standards that can be broken into further subsets. What are the main concepts you want your students to understand deeply? Begin your competency statements with either of these two constructs:

- ▶ Students will understand that . . .
- ▶ Students will demonstrate the ability to . . .

The other difference between a competency and a standard is that a competency is meant to be a higher-order demand. In our work, as I discuss later in this chapter, we validate competencies to make sure they are demanding, aligned to standards, concept-based, and assessable.

For example, the Common Core standard for understanding numbers and operations in base 10 reads as follows: "Recognize that in a multi-digit number, a digit in one place represents 10 times as much as it represents in the place to its right and 1/10 of what it represents in the place to its left."[2]

While this standard is important in the development of math skills, it does not rise to the level of a competency. To reach competency, the student must apply or transfer what they know and have learned in base 10 understanding. Simply recognizing number representation is neither a performance nor an application of high cognitive demand.

The following competency statement covers the same standard:" Students will expand their understanding of number systems, thinking flexibly, and attend to precision and reasonableness when solving problems using rational numbers."[3] This statement is more expansive and higher level than the Common Core standard. The cognitive demand, by virtue of requiring that the student think flexibly and attend to precision and reasonableness *when solving problems*, invokes higher cognitive demand than the standard, which only demands recognizing number representations. This competency statement invites performance criteria—or performance indicators—for assessment.

In designing good academic competencies, we need to make sure that every competency statement is carefully crafted and further aligned and articulated across the learning continuum. Take the time to look across your curriculum and not just within a grade level. If the goal of a student's learning journey is to move on when proficiency is demonstrated, the competencies must be designed for that purpose. In the traditional curriculum, standards are generally hardwired into specific grade levels. But if learners are moving at their own pace, academic competencies and their associated learning progressions cannot be assigned to a grade level. Think of taking grade-level curriculum, then lifting it out of the constraints of grade level, and going further in ratcheting up the rigor with tasks that are cognitively demanding. In the past few years, we have considered standards as the be-all and end-all of teaching. Shifting from coverage of content standards to focus more on cognitive demand is an important step in developing the CBE framework. Essentially, we need to rethink the grain size of what we traditionally have used in standards-based curricula to a larger grain size—that of concept-based statements of competency.

Next Charter School in Derry, New Hampshire, for example, began designing its innovative school as a competency-based, project-based, non-course-based high school by constructing its academic graduation competencies and personal success skills needed for graduation. Students must meet competencies such as social engagement and leadership to graduate in addition to their academic competencies that are embedded into the design of their projects. In "Voices from the Field: Next Charter School, Derry, New Hampshire," Justin Krieger and Joe Crawford, codirectors of Next, explain how they created this unique CBE high school.

VOICES FROM THE FIELD

NEXT CHARTER SCHOOL, DERRY, NEW HAMPSHIRE

By Joe Crawford and Justin Krieger, Codirectors of Next Charter School

The system of and for learning at Next Charter School is rooted in the following assumptions:

- One size does not fit all.
- All learners learn at different rates.
- There are an infinite number of pathways to learning.
- Learners must make meaning for themselves.

In the background, the instructional and assessment model at Next operates in a manner that posits that *the ongoing goal of education is student performance, not merely the acquisition of information*. To this end, much of the work we ask of students at Next emphasizes the act of *doing*—using their knowledge.

We define our curriculum as the gap between where the student is and where they need to go. Learning at Next, therefore, is individualized. Each student maintains his or her own pathway to graduation. However, this is not to propose that all learning is optional. While these pathways are infinitely flexible, they are aligned to an established set of goals identified as competency statements. Competencies are relevant and enduring statements that require students to use knowledge and skills to accomplish outcomes. Moreover, they are broad, content-related statements derived from state and national standards that promote the transfer of knowledge and skills to authentic, real-world applications. Students demonstrate their learning through project work that culminates in a product or performance that directly aligns with one or more competency statements. Students in this pursuit engage in feedback cycles with respective staff to refine their work until it meets competency. Students are not penalized or rewarded for time spent; nor is their achievement calculated using the mean or average. Instead, students use their time to improve their product or performance, and their achievement is recorded with a binary measure—they are either attempting to meet the competency, or they have met the competency. This act of reporting student achievement as met or not yet met emphasizes quality over quantity, and depth over breadth.

At Next, students align their education with individual goals and aspirations they currently hold or may hold in their respective futures. In collaboration with their advisor, students develop an individual learning plan (ILP) that organizes curriculum around meaningful learning experiences that are directly aligned to competencies. This flexible approach allows students to design and monitor the pace, order, and structure of their competency work. In a very real sense, the student designs a graduation pathway, and the role of Next is to unconditionally support the student along that pathway. This model is more akin to an à la carte menu than selecting one entrée from three for an upcoming wedding reception. This plan must remain a living document, subject to revisions at each ILP meeting. A student's ILP reflects not only the learning done in school, but also any credits earned through extended learning opportunities (ELOs). ELOs, experiences beyond the regular school day, typically fall under the direction of real-world experts. Students may earn credit for these supplemental activities when they work with Next staff members to align their experiences with competencies. To maintain a common, communicative language with other stakeholders in education, credit is awarded when a student meets all the competencies within a specific credit area.

Student performance is evaluated by comparing evidence of learning (student performance or product) against a performance- or product-specific rubric for all learning experiences. Competencies are met when the student's product or performance exhibits the established criteria communicated in the project rubric. Within a credit area, student progress is reported as a percentage of competencies completed. A student's progress toward the attainment of a high school diploma is reported as a percentage of all required competencies completed. Next Charter School uses an online grade-reporting software tool called JumpRope, which parents and students can use to track their competency attainment and progress toward graduation. This tool is a primary component of ILP progress meetings, which are generally held after each twenty-day project module and include the student, family, and advisor. Considering the dynamic nature of achievement, these individualized meetings allow stakeholders to have a conversation about student achievement in relation to the student's immediate and future goals.

The student experience at Next is analogous to driving a car. Performance matters. And one learns to perform through a series of unconditionally supported attempts to reach a level of competency within a given domain.

Next Charter School began its design work with the end in mind and worked backward. It unpacked its graduation competencies into performance indicators of increasing complexity and then used a project-based curriculum to engage students and determine which performance indicators and competencies were met over time. The performance indicators are clustered into course equivalents for the purpose of granting course credit. While Next's design is unique, it had the opportunity to design a public high school using a clean slate. In contrast, many schools in the public arena must overcome barriers that exist in their current structure in curriculum and instruction. To begin building the competency foundation of your school, you should understand what constitutes strong competency statements.

START AT THE BEGINNING: GOOD COMPETENCIES

As a general guideline in determining the number of competencies, educators should formulate the major concepts in the content area under discussion. Laying a sound groundwork for the number of competencies needed within a discipline will help when it is time to move to competency-based grading. A common number is four to eight academic competencies per grade level or high school course. In your curriculum, competencies will be further delineated within grade levels and courses, according to the appropriate instructional, learning, and assessment targets based on academic standards.

Between 2005 and 2008, New Hampshire high schools were required to develop course competencies and assessments to those competencies. As difficult as the task was to accomplish, it was made more difficult by the lack of guidance to help teachers distinguish between course content and competencies or exactly what a competency statement should look like. There was such variability in the number of competencies per course and the actual statements themselves that the New Hampshire Department of Education provided leadership and guidance to the field by calling together a group of high school teachers from a variety of content areas to create a tool for teachers to use when designing competency statements.

To give the best field guidance for teachers to design high-quality competency statements, we developed the *competency validation rubric* (table 3.1). This tool is meant to help test the quality of a competency statement. We looked closely at the content of the rubric, its clarity in communicating to a variety of teachers, its practicality, and its technical quality and fairness.[4] Ideally, the competency statements should be written and validated in a professional learning community or with at least one other educator within the same discipline.

We chose four dimensions of examining a competency statement using the rubric: (1) the relevance of the statement to the content area; (2) the *enduring concept*, or big idea, within the content area; (3) the statement's cognitive demand as measured by Webb's depth-of-knowledge criteria or Hess's cognitive-rigor matrices (or both); and (4) performance assessment considerations for the competency statement. In guiding teachers on how to use the tool, we considered a total score for a competency statement unimportant. For each dimension in the competency validation rubric, we created a prompt or an essential question to guide the teachers who were reviewing the competency statement. If a statement scored a 1 or a 2 on any dimension, it probably needed some reworking. If a statement scored a 3 or 4 on any dimension, it represented a strong statement in that regard.

The competency validation rubric is a good quality assurance tool if you are writing competency statements from scratch. Because many New Hampshire schools have designed competencies for their learning systems, many competencies are posted on school websites. To gain better insight into what strong

TABLE 3.1 Competency validation rubric

COMPETENCY DIMENSION	COMPETENCY STATEMENT AND SCORE			
	4 (Strongest statement)	3	2	1 (Weakest statement)
Relevance to content area: To what extent does this competency statement align with standards, leading students to conceptual understanding of content?	▪ Aligns with national, state, and/or local standards/frameworks; areas may be combined or clustered for learning. ▪ Articulates, in a clear and descriptive way, what is important in understanding the content area. ▪ Connects the content to higher concepts across content areas.	▪ Aligns with national, state, and/or local standards/frameworks; areas may be combined or clustered for learning. ▪ States what is important in understanding the content area. ▪ Addresses conceptual content.	▪ As beginning alignment with national, state, and/or local standards/frameworks. ▪ Is either too abstract or too specific in its content-area focus. ▪ Is so detailed in language that it obscures the connection to higher concepts.	▪ Has little evidence of alignment with standards or frameworks. ▪ Focus on content is factual, without connection to concepts.
Enduring concepts: To what extent does this competency statement reflect enduring concepts?	▪ Includes skills that are transferable across content areas and applicable to real-life situations. ▪ Requires an understanding of relationships between/among theories, principles, and/or concepts.	▪ Includes skills that are transferable across content areas with real-life connections. ▪ Is based on concepts supported by topics and/or facts.	▪ Is a statement specific to program/resource used. ▪ Is based on topics applicable to the course.	▪ Is limited to scope and sequence of textbook/program/resource. ▪ Is very specific to facts in content.

COMPETENCY STATEMENT AND SCORE			
COMPETENCY DIMENSION	**4 (Strongest statement)**	**3**	**2**	**1 (Weakest statement)**
Cognitive demand: What depth of knowledge does this competency statement promote?	▪ Requires deep understanding of content as well as application of knowledge to a variety of settings. ▪ Asks students to create conceptual connections and exhibit a level of understanding that is beyond the stated facts or literal interpretation and defend their position or point of view through application of content. ▪ Promotes complex connections through creating, analyzing, designing, proving, developing, or formulating.	▪ Reflects academic rigor and implies opportunities for students to apply knowledge in a variety of ways. ▪ Asks students to create conceptual connections and exhibit a level of understanding that is beyond the stated facts or literal interpretation. ▪ Promotes deep knowledge using reasoning, planning, interpreting, hypothesizing, investigating, or explaining.	▪ Is limited in academic rigor and/or opportunities to apply knowledge. ▪ Asks students to show what they know in ways that limit their ability to build conceptual knowledge. ▪ Requires engagement of mental practices such as identifying, defining, constructing, summarizing, displaying, listing, or recognizing.	▪ Asks for routine or rote thinking or basic recall, and lacks opportunities to apply knowledge. ▪ Asks students to show what they know in simplistic ways. ▪ Requires recall of information, facts, definitions, and terms; activities include reciting, stating, recognizing, listing, reproducing, memorizing or performing simple tasks or procedures.
Performance assessment: To what extent does the competency statement promote opportunities for students to demonstrate evidence of learning?	▪ Defines in clear and descriptive language what is to be measured. ▪ Promotes multiple and varied opportunities to demonstrate evidence of learning in interdisciplinary fashion.	▪ Defines what is to be measured. ▪ Promotes either multiple or varied opportunities to demonstrate evidence of learning.	▪ Is disconnected from the product of learning. ▪ Implies limited opportunities to demonstrate evidence of learning.	▪ Lacks description of what is to be measured. ▪ Limits evidence of learning to recall.

Source: New Hampshire Department of Education, "Competency Validation Rubric," 2010, www.education.nh.gov/innovations/hs_redesign/documents/validation_rubric.pdf.

competencies look like, consider the New Hampshire K–12 model English language arts (ELA) competencies.[5] Each competency has been validated by a network of teachers using the competency validation rubric:

1. *Reading literature*: Students will demonstrate the ability to comprehend, analyze, and critique a variety of increasingly complex print and nonprint literary texts.

2. *Reading informational texts*: Students will demonstrate the ability to comprehend, analyze, and critique a variety of increasingly complex print and nonprint informational texts—including texts for science, social studies, and technical subjects.

3. *Writing arguments*: Students will demonstrate the ability to analyze and critique texts or topics and support claims and reasoning with sufficient evidence for intended purpose and audience.

4. *Explanatory writing*: Students will demonstrate the ability to effectively write informative texts to examine and convey complex ideas for a variety of purposes and audiences.

5. *Narrative writing*: Students will demonstrate the ability to effectively apply narrative strategies for a variety of purposes and audiences.

6. *Research*: Students will engage in research/inquiry to investigate topics and to analyze, integrate, and present information.

7. *Listening*: Students will demonstrate the ability to listen and view critically for variety of purposes.

8. *Speaking*: Students will demonstrate the ability to speak purposefully and effectively—strategically making decisions about content, language use, and discourse style.

9. *Technology*: Students will demonstrate the ability to use the tools of technology (including digital media and the Internet) to gather, interpret, and analyze information and create sharable products.

Different schools and districts use these (and other content area) model competencies in a variety of ways. Some districts use some or all these competencies as their ELA competency statements in each grade level of K–12. The compe-

For progression see p. 44

tency statements are the same for each grade level. Each of the competencies then becomes the umbrella for the grade-level curriculum structure. The schools essentially organize their grade-level curriculum according to these umbrella competency statements. Doing so allows the schools to see their curriculum development across grade levels. Some schools also use these competencies as the foundation of their CBE grading system—the same competencies are used on report cards across the grade levels.

Some schools or districts begin with the model competencies as their formal grade-level and content-area competencies but then take these competencies into their units of instruction, customize them to the particular content, and possibly write them in student-friendly language. When you are designing competency statements, it is important to think of the overall architecture. Make sure they are strong statements, and know how you are going to use them in your assessment and grading systems.

Learning Progressions

Before learners can show that that they can apply their knowledge and skill, they first must learn the defined content and particular skills. If we are going to lift curriculum out of grade levels for students to learn at their own pace, we need to set out a progression of learning for them to support their advancement toward competency. In other words, we need to include learning progressions.

The term *learning progressions* has come to mean different things to different entities. Some groups think of learning progressions as a set of standards laid out in steps. Another definition for learning progression is the ungraded curriculum that is packaged into an online curriculum. In their brief on learning progressions, Achieve, an independent, nonprofit education reform organization, found that the term *learning progressions* may be defined differently by various experts.[6] Some will emphasize sequence and recognition of learning progress. Others define learning progression as a description of knowledge changing over time. Hess's research on learning progressions has informed the most recent development of the K–8 competencies in New Hampshire. We were fortunate to have Hess facilitate the latest development of ELA, mathematics, and science competencies in 2015–2016. Hess observes that learning progressions must be both research and evidence based.

The learning progression should demonstrate increasing complexity in the deeper and broader understanding of a big idea within a discipline. Hess also stresses the need to align well-designed assessments.[7]

Using Learning Progressions in CBE

The best way to illustrate the importance of incorporating learning progressions is to consider their development arc. A learning progression goes far beyond just thinking through a sequence of content standards. For example, an important concept in math is symbolic expression, yet it isn't defined as an anchor standard in the Common Core State Standards in Mathematics. The understanding of symbolic expression and its use increases with complexity across a math curriculum. Measurement is another big concept in mathematics. When I was recently working with a school in Dallas, the K–2 teachers were describing their integrated approach to learning math. They described how their little ones measure everything throughout the year because early learning is so experiential and integrated. I encouraged them to continue to think of it that way and to develop their instruction to the measurement math competency across the content disciplines throughout the year. I recommended they make sure they were capturing the need for different measurement strategies in their units of instruction across the year. In this way, they could ensure learning experiences that represented a learning progression in measurement. Their curriculum maps will be more authentic and will enable students to move along the learning progression to develop the concept of measurement.

For example, in New Hampshire's nationally aligned mathematics competencies for K–8, the learning progressions are shown in grade spans by their conceptual development (tables 3.2 and 3.3). Note how the complexity increases as the progression develops across the grade spans.

As shown, these competencies are represented with "I can" statements spanning a couple grades. The use of grade spans begins to dispel the thinking that all curricula are grade-level based. Simply put, depending on a student's prior knowledge and proficiencies, the child may be beyond or unable to perform at his or her assigned grade level. By honoring the grade-span development of a concept, learners can be assessed more readily against a learning progression to determine

TABLE 3.2 NH nationally aligned k-8 mathematics competencies

	K–2	3–4	5–6	7–8
1. Competency statements for foundations of math–symbolic expression "I can" statements are models of what educators may see in performance tasks when students demonstrate their increasin understanding and use of the competencies.	**Students will reason abstractly and quantitatively, reporting and making appropriate use of mathematical symbols and expressions for different purposes.** ■ I can represent whole-number quantities in multiple ways (words, symbols, expressions, equations, etc.) ■ I can interpret and explain conceptual meanings of mathematical relationships and symbols used for them, such as expressing quantities, equivalence, and greater than or less than. ■ I can represent and interpret addition and subtraction in multiple formats, including expressions and equations.	**Students will reason abstractly and quantitatively, recognizing and making appropriate use of mathematical symbols and expressions for a variety of purposes, including variables.** ■ I can represent whole-number decimal, and fractional quantities in multiple ways (with words, symbols, models, symbols, expressions, equations, etc.). ■ I can interpret and explain conceptual meanings of mathematical relationships and symbols used for them, such as expressing or comparing quantities, equivalence, etc. ■ I can represent and interpret the four operations in multiple formats, including expressions and equations.	**Students will reason abstractly and manipulate symbolic expressions to represent relationships and interpret expressions and equations in terms of a given context for determining an unknown value.** ■ I can symbolically represent relationships involving non-negative rational numbers, such as equivalent expressions, equations, inequalites, ordered pairs, inverse operations, ratio relationships, and exponents. ■ I can interpret and apply the use of vaired symbols in mathematical relationships, formulas, expressions, and operations. ■ I can provide mathematical justification when using or manipulating expressions, equations, or inequalities.	**Students will reason abstractly and manipulate symbolic expressions to represent relationships and interpret expressions and equations in terms of a given context for determining an unknown value.** ■ I can symbolically represent relationships involving irrational numbers, such as equivalent expressions, equations, inequalites, ordered pairs, inverse operations, exponents, and absolute value. ■ I can interpret and apply the use of vaired symbols in mathematical relationships, formulas, expressions, and operations. ■ I can provide mathematical justification when using or manipulating expressions and modeling linear equations (e.g., slope, rate of change) and inequalities.
Aligned national standards	KCC5, 1OA1, 2OA1, KCC6, 1NBT3, 2NBT4, KOA1, 1OA2, 2NBT7	3NF2, 4OA2, 3NF3, 4OA1, 3OA8, 4OA3, 3OA3, 4OA3, 3OA3, 4OA2	5OA2, 6EE3, 5OA1, 6EE2, 5NF2, 6EE4	7EE1, 8EE2, 8EE3, 7EE4, 8EE6, 7RP2, 8EE5

Source: New Hampshire Department of Education, "New Hampshire College and Career Ready K-8 Mathematics Model Competencies." (July 14, 2016): http://education.nh.gov /innovations/hs_redesign/documents/math-k-8-2016.pdf

TABLE 3.3   NH Common Core State Standards-Aligned Mathematics Model Graduation Competencies.

9–12	
1. Competency statements for symbolic expression "I can" statements are examples of what educators may see in performance tasks when students demonstrate their increasing understanding and use of competencies.	**Students will reason abstractly and manipulate symbolic expressions and models to represent relationships and interpret expressions, equations, and inequalities in terms of a given context (including real-world phenomena) for determining unknown values.** ▪ I can write, apply, and provide a rationale for a mathematical model representing a given situation) e.g., linear, quadratic, exponential, trigonometric). ▪ I can analyze and symbolically represent complex numbers (both real and imaginary numbers). ▪ I can interpret and use symbols to express relationships and justify reasoning when solving problems (e.g., evaluating expressions; modeling equations, inequalities, systems of equations/inequalities). ▪ I can apply properties of arithmetic and algebra to simplify and manipulate symbolic expressions or models involving real/imaginary numbers. ▪ I can analyze and use the structure of expressions to generate equivalent forms which emphasize different properties of the quantity represented by the expression (e.g., factoring, completing the square, various linear/nonlinear forms). ▪ I can analyze, symbolically represent, and use vector and matrix quantities in problem solving.

Source: New Hampshire Department of Education, "New Hampshire Common Core State Standards-Aligned Mathematics Model Graduation Competencies." (2016): http://education.nh.gov/innovations/hs_redesign/documents/NEW HAMPSHIREModelMATHGraduationCompetenciesV.6.16.16.pdf.

exactly where they are. The child can then further develop that concept without having either to wait for peers to finish the unit of work or to move on to the next level in the curriculum without truly understanding the concept. Thinking through this framework can break through the time barrier of traditional teaching and learning. The greater challenge is not in designing the curriculum but in supporting the learner wherever he or she is in the learning progression. It is also a challenge to see the development of a concept beyond grade 8 because of course sequencing and content in a myriad of required core courses and electives.

Learning progressions are important because they form the foundation for the pathways students take in their learning. This is where one of the most important shifts in competency education takes place: the shift from the curriculum that is

KS.

taught and the curriculum that is learned. You may have heard the term *learned curriculum*. As a principal, I became more aware of a different meaning for the term. One year, I realized that teachers at one grade level were at different places in their curriculum delivery. I knew from frequent walk-throughs what the pacing looked like across the grade. By the end of the year, some teachers had clearly reached the end of the district curriculum while others had not. That situation alone redefined the meaning of *learned curriculum*. Essentially, students didn't and couldn't learn a curriculum that wasn't taught, and some curriculum that was taught was certainly not learned by each student. Yet, at the beginning of the next school year, each of those students was introduced to the next grade-level curriculum as if each child had been taught it and had learned it.

Because of this disconnect between taught and learned, we educators actually create many of the problems that exist in learning expectations in our classrooms every day. To make things more complicated, we have devised all sorts of intervention systems when students cannot learn a particular grade-level curriculum. For example, take a sixth-grade student who cannot meet the learning targets for the sixth-grade reading curriculum. That student may then go into some sort of intervention time either alone or in small groups to address that gap. However, it may very well be that what prevents the student from successfully learning this curriculum may actually be a learning target that the student never met or was never taught in an earlier grade level.

In a competency-based learning environment, students learn at their own pace, demonstrating proficiency along the way. In many respects, a learner-centered approach allows for better allocation of teaching and funding resources. Chapter 6 will further consider the implications of designing learner support in competency-based learning.

Academic Competency Mapping

Once competency statements and learning progressions have been established, curriculum units and courses must be aligned to them. When we think of the journey that students take within an academic discipline from kindergarten to grade 12, we must be sure that it is a coherent one that increases with complexity along the way. One way to do this is to use a mapping strategy with any given competency. Using the New Hampshire ELA model competencies, the learning progression for the competency on informational text is as follows:[8]

> *Kindergarten–2*: Students will make meaning of increasingly complex informational print and nonprint texts, and provide text details to explain interpretations and thinking.
>
> *Grades 3–4*: Students will make meaning of increasingly complex informational print and nonprint texts, and provide text details to support interpretations and analyses.
>
> *Grades 5–6*: Students will comprehend and draw conclusions about the author's intent in a variety of increasingly complex print and nonprint informational texts, citing textual evidence to support their analyses.
>
> *Grades 7–8*: Students will comprehend and draw conclusions about the author's intent in a variety of increasingly complex print and nonprint informational texts, citing a range of relevant and compelling textual evidence to support their analyses.
>
> *High school*: Students will demonstrate the ability to comprehend, analyze, and critique a variety of increasingly complex print and nonprint informational texts—including texts for science, social studies, and technical subjects.

Note the increasing complexity of the competency statements as informational text is developed within the curriculum from kindergarten to grade 12.

Despite the nice, logical progression in these competency statements, how can we guarantee that the student has in fact had the appropriate learning experiences in informational text? To develop a coherent competency, you need competency mapping. The best approach for developing competency maps is to begin by organizing and reviewing your current curriculum by discipline area. You may find that your curriculum is poorly organized or that it has gaps. If that is the case, you will have to address this issue. Try to begin this work with the most coherent curriculum possible. Beyond banks of standards that may be assigned to grade levels, it is important to analyze where these standards are addressed in the units of instruction at each grade level. If your current curriculum is not organized into units of instruction using UbD or some other district template, it is important to take the time to agree on what units of instruction should be part of the curriculum for each grade level. With this curriculum map and a description of each unit, you can begin organizing your curriculum against competencies.

If you currently have a program in place across several grade levels and you intend to continue using the program in the future, use the program resources for your mapping. In my own experience, I have found that high school courses present the greatest difficulty in developing competency maps when the high school curriculum has not been organized for course content. In several situations that I have experienced, the high school staff needed to have some uncomfortable conversations among themselves about what they were teaching in their courses. In one large high school, for example, seven teachers taught the same US history course, using the same course description. The department members agreed on the ten competency statements for the social studies department. It should therefore have been a relatively easy exercise to line up the topics of their course units of instruction with the ten competencies. However, when each teacher created a concept map of his or her course units and the topics of each unit, there was no agreement. It opened up a very uncomfortable conversation with them. They didn't need to agree on how they taught their course, but they did need to agree on the major learning outcomes that every student should experience by virtue of taking the US history course in that school and to determine exactly what competencies are addressed in the course.

For high schools, this mapping exercise is an important one to ensure college and career readiness. In working with several high schools, we created coherence across the discipline by doing the following:

- Adopt or adapt the New Hampshire model competencies.
- For each course, using the chart in table 3.4, map which competencies are addressed in the units of instruction for the course.
- Examine the course mapping for the required courses for graduation.
- All competencies should be addressed within the core required curriculum.
- If there are gaps, address them through the units of instruction.
- If some competencies are overemphasized, remove the redundancies or overtaught topics in the required courses.

The mapping tool in table 3.4 is a user-friendly way to look across a curriculum from K to grade 12. By mapping the competencies using this tool, teachers can see where there are redundancies and gaps in the curriculum. I used ELA competencies in particular to show how other content-area teachers can easily map the coursework that draws on any of these competencies. Teachers in other disciplines can simply add their courses and units to the far left column. This is a good way to map competencies from several subject areas when using a project-based learning or multidisciplinary approach. For example, the potential to assess a student for an information-text competency via social studies or science can be powerful in breaking down course boundaries and can make earning credit more accessible. A humanities course, for example, can easily integrate English and social studies competencies, and students come to understand that research, reading, writing, and social studies are inexorably connected conceptually.

For another example, competencies that address each of the major concepts in science across the traditional courses in life science, earth and space science, and physical science should offer students varied opportunities to apply discipline-specific content and skills when the competencies are mapped across the required core courses leading to graduation. Opening up a curriculum to this type of cross-walking more accurately shows the varied opportunities any student has to meet competencies.

Mapping competencies across grade levels and courses has an added benefit in shaping the foundation of a competency-based grading system. Mapping competencies will reveal which competencies have greater importance.

Many schools and districts have uniformly committed to using UbD in developing their units of study for K–12.[9] This tool is especially helpful in the mapping process for competencies. High-quality unit design using UbD principles provides the strong structural documentation that helps educators understand the nature of competency design. This will also inform weighting decisions in building competency-based grading procedures.

Figure 3.1 shows the first part (the competency statements, or UbD stage 1) of a simplified template of how a competency-based course unit would be designed, using UbD principles. Inherent in the design of this template is an explicit connection of the learning unit learning to the whole-course or grade-level set of competencies.

TABLE 3.4   Competency mapping tool

List the units of instruction in each of the courses within your department. Use an X to denote which competencies are addressed in each unit of instruction. Title each unit appropriately. C = competency.

	C1	C2	C3	C4	C5	C6	C7	C8	C9
Course title									
Unit title									
Unit title									
Unit title									
Unit title									
Unit title									
Course title									
Unit title									
Unit title									
Unit title									
Unit title									
Unit title									
Course title									
Unit title									
Unit title									
Unit title									
Unit title									
Unit title									

FIGURE 3.1 Simplified template for a CBE unit of study, part 1: competency statements

Title of unit: Length of unit:

Teacher:

Course:

Previous unit:

Next unit:

COMPETENCY STATEMENTS		
List course/grade-level competencies: *(Use the construct: "Students will understand that . . ." or "Students will demonstrate the ability to . . . [depth of knowledge level 3 or 4].")*	**Unit competencies** *(Tag each competency to the course/grade-level competencies.)*	
	Essential question(s) *(Should be provocative, having more than one answer.)*	
	Acquisition of content knowledge and skill *(Notate and cite in a full statement for each standard.)*	
	Students will know . . .	Students will be skilled at . . .

Some users of this template code and number each of the course or grade-level competencies. They then use the coding to cross-reference the competencies in the unit. In the following example, the Epping School District in Epping, New Hampshire, has adapted its UbD templates to CBE and has mapped its customized course competencies to its district competencies. The following list of competencies is an example of a syllabus from a biology course. Each of the course competencies is mapped to the district competencies as part of its UbD template that was adapted for CBE course design.[10]

Epping District K–12 Science Competencies

Nature of science: Students will develop an appreciation for the role science plays in our culture and everyday lives, and actively engage in scientific investigation.

Stability and change: Students will understand that living things, materials, and systems remain constant, change at different rates, or exist in equilibrium over time.

Systems, energy, and matter: Students will understand that there is order and predictability in the universe, which can be organized into systems and energy.

Structure and function: Students will understand that the form or shape of a living thing, material, or system is related to its function.

Models and explanations: Students will understand that scientists use logic, models, evidence, and current knowledge to explain their world.

Biology course competencies mapped or tagged to district competencies:

1. Students will understand that scientific investigations are carried out under the guidelines of the scientific method through the safe and proper use of the tools and technology of the trade. *(Nature of science, models, and explanations)*

2. Students will understand that the cell is the basic unit of life for all living things and it is at the cellular level where organisms meet all the necessary requirements to sustain life. *(Structure and function, systems, energy and matter)*

3. Students will understand that DNA that is handed down through populations determines the genetic structure of all individuals and

that differences in the DNA patterns are responsible for genetic diversity. *(Stability and change, systems, energy and matter)*

4. Students will understand that organisms are classified into a system of kingdoms according to their degree of evolutionary relatedness. *(Stability and change, structure and function)*

5. Students will understand that species evolve over time through the process of natural selection based on genetic variation and environmental factors. *(Stability and change, models and explanations)*

6. Students will understand that ecosystems are made up of interrelated populations and that the actions of the individuals within any species can have an impact on the survival of the entire ecosystem. *(Structure and function, systems, energy and matter)*

7. Students will understand that matter and energy flow through and between ecosystems following patterns that include both living and nonliving factors. *(Systems, energy and matter, structure and function)*

8. Students will understand that scientific knowledge is the result of the cumulative efforts of people, past and present, who have attempted to understand the natural world, and that this knowledge is continually revised as new information is obtained. *(Nature of science, models and explanations)*

Each course syllabus uses the UbD template to further describe and map each unit of instruction to the course-level competencies above. Customizing the course-level competency statements makes them more relevant to both the teacher and the students. It also gives guidance to the teacher in recording assessment grades by pointing to which competency the grade should be entered under. From a district perspective, when the courses with their units of instruction are mapped to the district competencies, the district has a K–12 overview of which science competencies are addressed across each grade or course in the district.

Designing school and district competencies and mapping competencies to units of instruction is foundational work in the CBE framework. It lays the groundwork for designing appropriate performance assessments and your competency-based grading system.

Chapter 4

Personal Success Skills

DISPOSITIONS, NONCOGNITIVE SKILLS, *soft skills*, *twenty-first-century skills*—all these terms refer to a group of qualities we know are important for success in life. As we shift from traditional structure to competency-based learning systems, we should also honor the skills and qualities that can be even more important in the long term for success in life.

Recently, while I was facilitating a vision-setting activity with a group of high school parents, they spoke confidently about the fine education their kids were receiving at their high school. They felt assured that their children would gain all the skills necessary for success by the time they graduated from high school. I pressed them: How did they know this? My question caused a bit of a buzz in the room. I pressed them further and asked how the school was communicating their child's development of these qualities. This school's report card is traditional and course based. It also reports on a few nonacademic areas that the teachers assess at the end of every term. Coincidentally, those nonacademic areas were not on the parents' list of what it takes to get that handshake at graduation in the vision-setting exercise. This disconnect between what parents had listed and what is truly needed for college and career readiness was a great opportunity for the principal to speak about why the school was moving forward to prepare their children for life beyond high school. The principal explained that the school was developing better ways to teach, assess, and communicate their child's progress both in academics and in the other qualities that are so important for success in life.

As mentioned earlier in the book, I speak of these other qualities important in life as *personal success skills*. This term resonates more easily with parents and educators. They simply get it. Although personal success skills can also be taught, learned, and assessed along the K–12 learning journey, they are quite different from academic skills. Ellen Hume-Howard, curriculum co-coordinator for the Sanborn Regional School District in Kingston and Newton, New Hampshire, describes them as the students' skills that define who they are as individuals. From the day a student walks through the doors of a classroom, we as educators should work with and develop these skills—the kids' sets of personal assets.

Personal success skills have been left out of the Common Core State Standards documents but are implied as part of the college- and career-readiness profile. When Common Core standards are part of a cognitively demanding learning activity, their rigor would certainly require students to learn to persevere through difficult and complex reasoning skills. Yet, it is hard to pinpoint exactly what those college- and career-readiness skills—like persistence—are and how we must address them across the K–12 continuum in various teaching and learning opportunities.

Fortunately, a number of researchers have identified skills that are linked to college and career readiness and that we can infuse into the learning process. One of the best resources for understanding college and career readiness in your CBE planning is David Conley's work. Conley describes four keys to college and career readiness: cognitive strategies, content knowledge, learning skills, and transition knowledge and skills.[1] His work is a good primer for thinking through how to shift current teaching and learning experiences to emphasize the techniques and strategies that are essential to readiness for the future. Table 4.1 further explains each of the keys.

The work of Karin Hess and Brian Gong reinforces Conley's findings in identifying readiness for college and career.[2] Their model is most helpful for educators trying to shift from traditional instructional models to competency-based teaching and learning. Hess and Gong identify three skill sets needed for college and career readiness (figure 4.1).

TABLE 4.1 Four keys to college and career readiness

KEY SKILLS	DESCRIPTION
Cognitive strategies	These strategies include problem formulation, research, interpretation, communication, precision, and accuracy. These ways of thinking are necessary for students to think independently as part of their college-level work.
Content knowledge	Content knowledge includes structural knowledge of content: the key organizing concepts, linking ideas, and terminology; technical knowledge and skills; and attitudes toward learning content. In understanding the structure of knowledge in core subjects, students are better able to retain their learning and make conceptual connections across their learning. In developing their content knowledge, students should come to know what they need to learn to follow a career pathway and discern how they are they are moving toward competency.
Learning skills	Student ownership of learning and specific learning techniques covers a broad variety of personal skills that may be defined in part by a student's ability to self-direct, persist, develop self-awareness, monitor progress (metacognitive skills, that is, thinking about thinking or the process of self-reflection on learning), and seek help. Other learning skills include students' abilities to manage their time, learn how to study, read strategically, and work collaboratively.
Transition knowledge and skills	This skill set enables students to navigate in the next phase of their lives. Awareness of the norms, culture, and financial aspects of their postsecondary experience is essential for success. To succeed and graduate from high school, students must be able to self-advocate in this new life experience and seek out role models. Developing the requirements and readiness for career pathways also is key to success in the postsecondary experience.

Source: Adapted from David T. Conley, "A Complete Definition of College and Career Readiness," Educational Policy Improvement Center, May 2, 2012, www.epiconline.org/ccr-definition.

The research by Conley; Hess and Gong; and others on college and career readiness affects the way we must now look at our traditional curriculum. Specifying standards as guideposts for teaching and learning alone is not enough. We must shift instructional design to provide rich learning opportunities that deeply engage students in a rigorous curriculum of cross-cutting skills, knowledge, and behaviors. Such a shift is a fundamental and perhaps galactic leap into redesigning how we have structured teaching and learning for the past few generations.

I often use Hess and Gong's pyramid depicted in figure 4.1 to exemplify how traditional curriculum designs of grade- or course-level content alone fall short of preparing students for college or the workforce. The illustration can be especially helpful when you are designing competency-based learning opportunities for students. The apex of the pyramid is that handshake at graduation: the ability of a student to persevere in challenging new learning opportunities and to be

FIGURE 4.1   Cross-cutting college- and career-readiness (CCR) skills

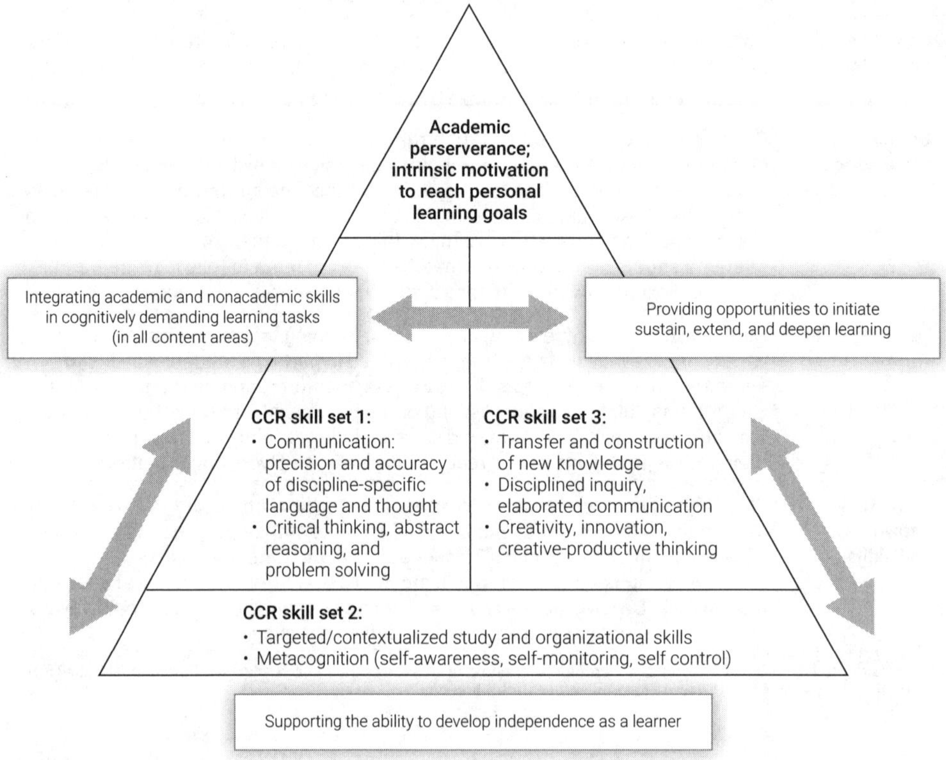

Academic
perserverance;
intrinsic motivation
to reach personal
learning goals

Integrating academic and nonacademic skills
in cognitively demanding learning tasks
(in all content areas)

Providing opportunities to initiate
sustain, extend, and deepen learning

CCR skill set 1:
• Communication:
  precision and accuracy
  of discipline-specific
  language and thought
• Critical thinking, abstract
  reasoning, and
  problem solving

CCR skill set 3:
• Transfer and construction
  of new knowledge
• Disciplined inquiry,
  elaborated communication
• Creativity, innovation,
  creative-productive thinking

CCR skill set 2:
• Targeted/contextualized study and organizational skills
• Metacognition (self-awareness, self-monitoring, self control)

Supporting the ability to develop independence as a learner

Source: Karin Hess and Brian gong, "Ready for College and Careet? Achieving the Common Core Standards and Beyond Through Deeper, Student-Centered Learning," National Center for the Improvement of Educational Assessment, March 2014, www.nmefoundation.org/getattachment/Resources/SCL-2/Ready-for-College-and-Career/Ready-for-College-and-Career.pdf?ext=.pdf. Used with permission.

intrinsically motivated to reach new learning goals. The base of the pyramid described as skill set 2 refers to the personal skill development comparable to Conley's key learning skills. Self-knowledge through metacognition (i.e., the students' self-reflection on their own learning) throughout the K–12 journey is foundational. As we will see when we develop learning pathways in the CBE framework (chapter 6), self-knowledge is at the heart of personalized learning.

Skill set 1 (comparable to Conley's cognitive strategies and content knowledge) is at core of the teaching and learning model in CBE. As teachers, we must design challenging learning opportunities and environments so that students can engage in critical thinking across content areas and can challenge their own thinking.

Skill set 3, including the ability to transfer and construct new knowledge, develops the independence in the learner by initiating, sustaining, and deepening learning. Providing students with this type of learning opportunity brings them to readiness and competence as they approach their higher-education learning experiences or the challenges of workforce settings.

Both Conley's and Hess and Gong's work reinforces the notion that competency education is far more than a list of standards. In fact, the key skills go far beyond the demand of any set of standards.

DEFINING YOUR PERSONAL SUCCESS SKILLS

The challenge ahead of you is to hone in on a set of success skills that have merit by being college- and career-readiness skills that your community values. For example, because Next Charter School values social engagement and leadership, it includes them in the personal success skills it reports on regularly leading up to graduation. Through the work of the Innovation Lab Network of the Council of Chief School State Officers (CCSSO), led by Sarah Lench, four essential skills have been identified as essential to college and career readiness: collaboration, communication, creativity, and self-direction.[3] These skills, which I recommend most often to define the personal success skills essential in college and career readiness, were also adopted by the state of New Hampshire in 2014 as personal success skills (called *work study practices* in New Hampshire) to be assessed by all districts. Their CCSSO's Innovation Lab Network's developmental framework breaks out each skill into inter- and intrapersonal dimensions across a continuum of development from beginner to advanced beginner to strategic learner to the last stage, the emerging expert ready for college and career choices. This framework can be consulted as you begin to build your continuum of college and career readiness.

The key to incorporating these developmental skills into your competency-based system is to recognize that they should be explicitly linked to learning opportunities within academic areas and to other opportunities that are part of school programming. For example, service opportunities and ELOs provide a wonderful setting for students to use their collaboration and self-direction skills. It is important for teachers to assess these skills as part of learning experiences, but it is most important for the students to reflect on and assess their own growth and the development of these skills over time. By including this self-reflection in their personal learning plans, students can be more self-aware of their assets and where they need further growth. In this way, assessment practices shift from being totally teacher centered to ones that include both teacher feedback and student self-assessment.

Although you may define a greater number of personal success skills than the four essential skills set forth by Lench previously, you will need to consider how you and the learner will track this developmental growth from kindergarten through grade 12. Consider the essential skill of collaboration. Think of all the opportunities where collaboration is part of academic and general school learning. The goal of designing the assessment system for the skill of collaboration should be to create a system, much like an open box, where the student and all the teachers across all the grade levels and content areas would deposit an assessment of the student's collaboration whenever the skill is used. Over time, these assessments are used to determine the student's growth over time against the developmental continuum, with scores such as beginner, advanced beginner, strategic learner, and emerging expert. At any point, you should be able to consider the student's collaboration box and see multiple scores contributed by multiple evaluators to determine where the student is on the developmental continuum for collaboration.

This approach diverges greatly from current approaches used in assessing noncognitive skills. Traditionally, it is the teacher who generally assesses the skills at the end of a school term, in time for the report card. Often, this assessment is given a score of 1, 2, 3, or 4, according to a general rubric that is teacher designed. Unfortunately, this student information remains linked to the teacher, a course, a content area, and a grade level. It is generally never linked to the same score made by other teachers in other disciplines or across the grade levels. The noncognitive skills that are typically found on traditional report cards include effort, motivation, and citizenship.

To design your college- and career-ready set of personal success skills, begin with collaboration, communication, creativity, and self-direction. These skills will be designed into the competency-based performance tasks in the academic content areas (see chapter 6). To that set, add any other skills that your community values for its graduates.

As you think through a system that needs to communicate growth over time in these areas, begin to think about how the system will integrate this information with grade reporting. Many learning management systems on the market today can do this work as part of a student's personal learning plan. Sometimes, adding a new system-wide learning management program is impossible.

Franklin High School, a small high school in Franklin, New Hampshire, with limited resources, has worked for many years making progress in its personalized CBE system. I worked closely with the members of the science department when they began to develop their competencies as part of a cohort of schools working on developing ELOs. They began their departmental competency work by having the same four competency statements used in each of their science courses. This set of competency statements was grounded in the nature of science, problem solving, modeling, and analytical thinking. Teachers took those statements into their courses and customized the competency statements. As their CBE system evolved, they continued to work on upgrading their course-level competency statements. The following are sample competency statements from several of their courses:

- ▸ Students will understand that energy is necessary for change to occur in matter and can be stored, transferred, and transformed, but cannot be destroyed.
- ▸ Students will understand that all stationary and moving objects are affected by forces.
- ▸ Students will demonstrate the ability to apply concepts learned to explain how theories, organisms, and matter change over time and that all matter is interrelated.
- ▸ Students will demonstrate the ability to identify, evaluate, and apply how energy and matter flow through a variety of systems.
- ▸ Students will understand that the atom is a discrete unit and that all reactions, properties, and identities of elements and compounds are a result of its structure.

► Students will understand that all matter and energy in the universe is constant, neither being created nor destroyed, only stored, transferred, or transformed.

► Students will understand that chemical reactions are affected by the physical conditions of the system, including energy, temperature, pressure, concentration, particle size, presence of a catalyst, and nature of the atom's reactivity based on its position on the periodic table.

When scoring student work, teachers score the appropriate science competency using its rubric along with the appropriate schoolwide competency, which speaks to the set of personal success skills Franklin High School has identified. Among these skills are the following:

► working independently and collaboratively
► responsibility, character, cultural understanding, and ethical behavior
► written communication skills
► reading and comprehension skills
► speaking and listening skills
► problem-solving skills

These schoolwide competencies have subsets of skills that are scored with rubrics. The key feature of this system is that the schoolwide competencies (personal success skills) are scored using the same evaluative criteria by all teachers and students.

Most school districts already have some pieces in place to begin designing a comprehensive system that grows with the student. When the Rochester, New Hampshire, School District began its high school competency-based grading work, it separated the academic and nonacademic reporting. The school used a professionalism rubric at the high school level to report on factors the district thought were important to fully communicate student behaviors. When grades K–8 developed their competency-based grading, the educators also wanted to communicate to parents the student behaviors that were important. However, the high school professionalism rubric was not appropriate for younger students. A group of K–12 educators met to design their rubric for habits of engaged learners; this rubric became part of the K–12 comprehensive grading system.

The Sanborn Regional School District had a similar situation. The two elementary schools used CARES (cooperation, assertion, responsibility, empathy, and self-regulation or self-control)—indicators based on student responsibility and civic-mindedness. The middle school used several general learning outcomes as indicators. The high school used schoolwide student expectations developed as part of its regional school accreditation plan. Sanborn chose to continue with its current system and then grow toward the New Hampshire work study practices. The school mapped its existing skills to the state's work study practices of collaboration, communication, creativity, and self-direction. Table 4.2 shows how the local skills sets are mapped to the essential college- and career-ready skills. Mapping your school's existing skills onto the skills your community or school envisions may be a strategy that you can use with the existing nonacademic dispositions in your district.

Another model for integrating personal success skills is provided by Making Community Connections (MC2) Charter School. The school was founded by Kim Carter, executive director of QED Foundation, a New Hampshire nonprofit that promotes and supports personalized, competency-based education. MC2 promotes the development of a framework of habits, essential knowledge, and college career readiness. Each student entering school builds an ILP based on the student's learning profile, which the school developed from a research-based learning and neurodevelopmental framework. Each student develops habits through his or her learning and through a great deal of reflection and engagement happens. Among the habits the school encourages are these:

community ownership	creative thinking
self-direction	communication
management	curiosity and wonder
collaboration	problem solving
quality work	organization
decision making	information technology
character	leadership
critical thinking	global leadership

TABLE 4.2 Sanborn Regional School District work study practices (personal success skills)

STATE OF NEW HAMPSHIRE WORK STUDY PRACTICES

Communication	Creativity	Collaboration	Self-direction
Use various media to interpret, question, and express knowledge, information, ideas, feelings, and reasoning to create mutual understanding.	Use original and flexible thinking to communicate ideas or construct a unique product or solution.	Work in diverse groups to achieve a common goal.	Initiate and manage learning through self-awareness, self-motivation, self-control, self-advocacy, and adaptability as a reflective learner.
Graduating seniors will be able to demonstrate that they can: • communicate effectively using multiple modalities • interpret information using multiple senses • demonstrate ownership of the work	Graduating seniors should be able to demonstrate that they can: • think originally and independently • take risks • consider alternate perspectives • incorporate diverse resources	Graduating seniors will be able to demonstrate that they can: • contribute respectfully • listen and share resources and ideas • accept and fulfill roles • exercise flexibility and willingness to compromise	Graduating seniors will be able to demonstrate that they can: • persevere in completing complex, challenging tasks • use self-reflection to influence work and goals • engage stakeholders to gain support

DISTRICT-WIDE HIGH SCHOOL GRADES 9–12, TWENTY-FIRST-CENTURY SKILLS

Effectively communicate	Creatively solve problems	Contribute to their community	Self-manage their learning	Produce quality work	Responsibly use information
Use various media to interpret, question, and express knowledge, information, ideas, feelings, and reasoning to create mutual understanding.	Use original and flexible thinking to communicate ideas or construct a unique product or solution.	Work in diverse groups to achieve a common goal.	Initiate and manage learning through self-awareness, self-motivation, self-control, self-advocacy, and adaptability as a reflective learner.	Recognize and produce work of high quality.	Demonstrate a proficiency to effectively and ethically find and use information.

MIDDLE SCHOOL GRADES 6–8, GENERAL LEARNING OUTCOMES

Effectively communicate	Creatively solve problems	Contribute to their community	Self-manage their learning	Produce quality work	Responsibly use information
Use various media to interpret, question, and express knowledge, information, ideas, feelings, and reasoning to create mutual understanding.	Use original and flexible thinking to communicate ideas or construct a unique product or solution.	Work in diverse groups to achieve a common goal.	Initiate and manage learning through self-awareness, self-motivation, self-control, self-advocacy, and adaptability as a reflective learner.	Recognize and produce work of high quality.	Demonstrate a proficiency to effectively and ethically find and use information.

ELEMENTARY SCHOOL GRADES K–5, CARES

Cooperation	Assertion	Responsibility	Empathy	Self-regulation/control
▪ Work productively in a group. ▪ Display a positive attitude.	▪ Show initiative and effort. ▪ Seek help when it is needed. ▪ Participates in class. ▪ Demonstrate creativity, critical thinking, and problem-solving strategies.	▪ Work to the best of their ability. ▪ Complete assigned tasks. ▪ Complete homework.	▪ Show respect for others and their property. ▪ Show respect for others' opinions. ▪ Value the community of the classroom and school.	▪ Listen attentively. ▪ Follow school and classroom rules. ▪ Stay on task (stamina and perseverance). ▪ Demonstrate self-control in structured settings.

MC2 is a non-time-based democratic learning community, meaning that all the students have a voice in the governance of their school. MC2 students grow in their habits leading to graduation and only graduate when they have demonstrated they have met the required personal habits and academic competencies.

A DESIGN SCHEMA FOR PERSONAL SUCCESS SKILLS

Whether you use collaboration, communication, creativity, and self-direction as your only personal success skills or you use a wider variety of skills, a very important part of the design of your CBE framework is the skills' inclusion in the design of the performance tasks. By including the skills in this way, they will be assessed at the time of learning. The assessments of personal success skills should not be included in the assessment of the core content. The personal success skills are assessed separately with rubrics, and the scores are considered separately from the academic grading. This change in scoring and grading may start you on your path to designing a CBE grading system that communicates multiple dimensions of student learning and growth. Figure 4.2 is a design schema to keep in mind as you assess personal success skills as part of a competency-based learning activity.

FIGURE 4.2   Design schema for assessment of personal success skills

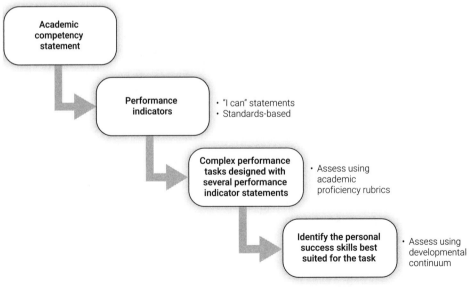

As we will see in chapter 5, designing performance assessments is essential to your CBE framework. As teachers develop their assessment literacy within this framework, they will come to value their ability to help their students develop personal success skills as part of the students' total growth toward college and career readiness.

Chapter 5

Performance Assessment

COMPETENCY REQUIRES STUDENTS to apply their knowledge and skills. The assessment of that application, or performance, determines competency. Thorough evaluations of competency must use various indicators. Such evaluations are a significant shift from traditional paper-and-pencil testing at the end of a chapter or a unit—the grade that relies on a single measure and that appears on the front page of the test. Educators need to make a substantial shift in their assessment and grading practices to move from a single measure to multiple indicators or evidence. Let's consider a framework that takes the best practices in the field of assessment and applies them to the performance assessment required in a competency-based learning environment. We'll connect assessment practices to grading in chapter 7.

The assessment of competencies in the CBE framework includes several steps:

- ▸ teacher-designed performance tasks with student demonstration of learning
- ▸ rubrics to assess student learning in performance tasks, with competency designated at the "strategic" thinking level (i.e., Webb's depth-of-knowledge level 3, which will be explained in this chapter)
- ▸ teacher-designed formative tasks that trigger relearning, and teacher-designed summative assessment when the student is ready
- ▸ assessments or demonstrations of learning that inform the evaluation of competency

DESIGNING COMPETENCY-BASED PERFORMANCE ASSESSMENTS

David Conley and Linda Darling-Hammond have shown that large-scale assessment tests do not adequately assess all the college- and career-readiness skills.[1] They describe the need for a continuum of assessments to best determine a student's college and career readiness. This continuum of assessments relies on multiple varied opportunities for students to apply their learning in unique, real-world learning tasks.

As we shift assessment practices from paper-and-pencil end-of-unit assessments to such assessments embedded in learning, we need to think about how students can demonstrate their ability to transfer the content and skills they have learned. If our aim is to prepare students for the real world, we need to give them the real world in school every day. This includes how they approach learning new concepts and how we, as educators, will evaluate them.

The traditional just-in-case curriculum (i.e., "just in case it's on the test" instruction) may fail in relevance and rigor. What would it look like for teachers to have competency in mind when creating real-world scenarios that, when presented at the beginning of a unit, hook the students into researching what they need to know to do the task? As much as this is a shift from just-in-case to just-in-time learning, it also provides a more realistic assessment of where students are in their learning, what they need to know to work the task, and, finally, whether they have met the performance criteria of the competencies (as indicated in a rubric) when they perform the task. This describes formative learning and summative assessment: the students find out what they need to know through research, and they practice new skills and then apply it to the real-world task before them. The product of this application is the summative assessment.

While I was visiting a school, a teacher told me that she was preparing her students for the Smarter Balanced Assessment Consortium (SBAC) testing that was looming in the not-too-distant future for her students. To prepare them, she had them work on the sample performance tasks. After I probed a bit further into why the teacher chose these tasks, she answered simply that if they could do the tasks, they would be prepared for the tasks on the SBAC testing date.

What was missing in the scenario above was the intentional design for learning. While the SBAC tasks are demanding and the students could learn a great deal from doing these tasks, it might have made more sense if the students had relevant, coherent learning before being given the SBAC sample assessment. Whether it is SBAC sample performance tasks or tasks created locally, each task should be authentic and connected to the current unit of study.

In some units of instruction, one performance task may be all that is needed to measure the competency. In other units, several smaller tasks may be planned into a unit of instruction as a better evaluation of student learning. Figure 5.1 illustrates the coherence created when the competencies within units of instruction are mapped to the course or grade-level competencies. With this framework, it is easy to see how the performance tasks across a course or a year are connected to each other and to the unit and course competencies. As the figure shows, the intentional design of high-quality performance tasks ensures valuable learning experiences and the effective assessments of competencies.

FIGURE 5.1   Coherence of competency-based course or grade curriculum

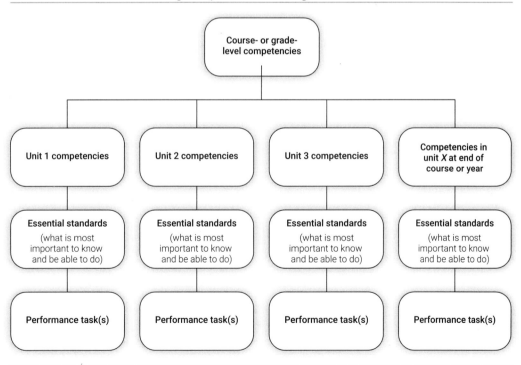

DESIGNING HIGH-QUALITY PERFORMANCE TASKS

When designing high-quality performance tasks, keep in mind several elements. Begin with a strong, validated competency statement. The next element in the design should be the unit of study that specifies the standards addressed in the learning outcomes for the unit. If you are using the UbD tool, review what you have identified as the essential content and skills associated with the unit. Take the content and skills standards, and apply a performance level using an "I can" statement. These are the performance indicators on which you will begin designing your performance tasks. You don't need a performance indicator for every standard; you can cluster some standards together into "I can" statements. These statements, which constitute the foundation of your formative and summative assessment system, are used by the students to guide the self-assessment of their learning. Many teachers use a performance indicator as an exit card that students complete. Doing so helps the teacher customize a student's need to spend more time the next day on the same topic or signals that the student is ready to move on. Formative learning and its assessments prepares the student for their summative performance where they must apply what they have learned. In the CBE framework, it is important to consider the cognitive demand of these performance indicators. Teachers should use Webb's depth-of-knowledge (DOK) criteria together with Hess's cognitive-rigor matrices when assigning the appropriate cognitive demand or DOK to each of the indicators.

DEPTH OF KNOWLEDGE

The level of complexity, or DOK, is one of the most important curricular considerations in CBE because it lays the groundwork for what must be learned and assessed. For students to apply their learning in complex, demanding ways, they need to *learn* in complex, demanding ways. Failure to do so results in the assessment gap: students are being assessed at a different level than the level at which they are learning. For example, a student may have good comprehension of a novel he or she is reading, but may perform poorly on a character analysis essay on the written test. If the student has not had the opportunity to analyze one or more characters as part of the unit of work leading up to the final written analysis question on the test, the child has fallen into the assessment gap. The student is being assessed on criteria for which he or she never learned: the elements of *writing* good character analysis.

While Norman Webb has provided the criteria for his four levels of DOK, teachers generally struggle with how these levels compare with Bloom's taxonomy.[2] I personally have set aside Bloom's taxonomy for a variety of reasons. In working with teachers, I have found that some interpret Bloom's as a progression in which students must move from the bottom to the top. The teachers sometimes even design their instruction that way. What can be a bit more insidious is how this type of thinking can influence how students are grouped. Students who are perceived as being unable to analyze at the "analyze" level of Bloom's taxonomy may be placed in a lower-level course. Regrettably, some schools base their student placement and academic instruction levels on these types of interpretations.

The purpose of categorizing the performance indicators by their DOK level is to ensure that students are learning content and acquiring skills—considered low DOK—but also that they are learning how to use these skills in higher-DOK performance indicators that require higher-order thinking skills—the hallmark of competency or proficiency.

The best tool for designing and assessing competency-based learning is Hess's cognitive-rigor matrices.[3] This tool helps teachers see how Bloom's taxonomy and Webb's DOK intersect.

For example, using the cognitive-rigor matrix for writing and speaking, Webb's DOK level 1 (recall and reproduction) would have students able to do the following:

▸ Apply rules or use other resources to edit for spelling, grammar, punctuation, style conventions, or word use.
▸ Apply basic formats for documenting sources.

Webb's DOK level 2 (skills and concepts) would have the students able to accomplish these tasks:

▸ Use context to identify or infer the intended meaning of words or phrases.
▸ Obtain, interpret, and explain information using text features (table, diagram, etc.).

▸ Develop a (brief) text that may be limited to one paragraph (e.g., a précis).

▸ Apply basic organizational structures (paragraph, sentence types, topic sentence, introduction, etc.) in writing.

Both DOK levels clearly call on the student to apply basic writing concepts or skills, but these applications have low complexity. They certainly are the tools of good writers, and we do expect our students to apply these tools in their writing. Tasks and products of learning at these two levels constitute formative learning and assessment. However, a higher level of complexity in writing is represented by the more complex cognitive demand of DOK levels 3 and 4.

Level 3 (strategic thinking and reasoning) involves using skills and concepts learned and fashioning them into writing products in ways that are not simply right or wrong, as in the DOK level 1 and 2 applications. The tasks in level 3 are much more strategic and include the following:

▸ Revise a final draft for meaning, progression of ideas, or the chain of logic.

▸ Apply internal consistency of text organization and structure to a full composition or oral communication.

▸ Apply a concept in a new context.

▸ Apply word choice, point of view, style, or other rhetorical devices to influence readers' interpretation of a text.

At level 4 in Webb's DOK (extended thinking), the student could accomplish these tasks:

▸ Select or devise an approach from many alternatives to research and present a novel problem or issue.

▸ Illustrate how multiple themes (historical, geographic, social, etc.) may be interrelated within a text or topic.[4]

As the DOK level increases, the complexity of an application, or task, increases. By applying content and skills in unique ways, a student demonstrates strategic thinking. At DOK levels 3 and 4, tasks and their assessments are summative and hence are true measures of proficiency or competence.

vs

Learning at DOK levels 1 and 2 represents low-level thinking involving factual content and skills acquisition. Generally, the students' answers are either right or wrong; either they know the answer or they don't. Because DOK levels 3 and 4 require that a student apply strategic and extended thinking, a student may be searching for the best answer, not just any answer. The higher level of complex thinking and reasoning leads to deeper learning that students can then take into future learning situations, where low-level information is often forgotten.

This attention to higher-level DOK in performance indicators is critical in the design of competency-based systems. Grading schemata and task rubrics must draw on the qualities found in strategic thinking, reasoning, and extended thinking to define proficiency or competency scales. I used the previous writing example to underscore this importance. How often do educators consider grammar and composition the only criteria for a good writing grade? The writing teacher may very well feel that students are applying the rules of writing and that, in and of itself, the students are at the *application* level in Bloom's taxonomy. But this level is clearly not enough to give the students the learning experiences they need to be good writers.

Sophistication = DOK 3-4

Professional development to help teachers understand the curricular implications of DOK is critical in the design of a CBE system and will add rigor to instruction and assessment as teachers take on a new perspective. Inherent in this work is also the need to question the rigor and complexity of many purchased curriculum programs, especially at the elementary level. When the Rochester School District began to examine its purchased K–6 math curriculum, the educators found some instruction and a great deal of assessment materials that were of such low-level cognitive demand (DOK levels 1 and 2) that the district had to go into the program materials and ratchet up the complexity of the instructional and assessment materials. The district used the mathematics cognitive-rigor matrix to rewrite math problems so that the responses were open-ended rather than simply right or wrong. It made sure that the assessment questions had a range of DOK levels to be sure the district could focus on the level 3 and 4 questions to determine whether the student met the competency. The DOK levels of the assessment questions matched the DOK levels of the instructional materials.

"load"

Understanding the implications of DOK or cognitive demand means a shift from traditional assessment to the design of performance assessment opportunities. High-quality performance tasks and their assessments provide the vehicle for student to both learn and be assessed at high levels.

Engaging Scenarios

As you unpack your competencies into performance indicators, think of bundling the performance indicators together into a task. Performance tasks put the student at the center of the learning and therefore should be the hook that engages them in wanting to know more about the topic. These engaging scenarios could be a problem that needs solving or a topic essential to the curriculum. One great tool that helps teachers develop expertise in designing engaging performance tasks is the RAFT strategy, which involves creating roles for the students, an audience, a format, and a topic.

Knowing that the task should hook students, teachers can conduct surveys of the students' preferences and interests to search for an appealing topic. Even without surveys, a graffiti board in a classroom or a conversation in an advisory (where a teacher meets regularly with a small group to advise students on academic, social, and career issues) can help a teacher design a high-interest topic for students to work into an engaging scenario.

A teacher can create several roles, audiences, and formats around a central topic to give students a choice and a voice in how they would like to demonstrate their learning. In approaching the design of learning this way, teachers new to this practice should start slowly and introduce fewer choices, then build toward more student choices in the RAFT.

The following sample performance tasks may give you some ideas for your own classroom:

► Your group has been tasked with designing the tile pattern for your sixth-grade hallway. You must collaborate in designing several color patterns for your classmates to vote on for their preference. Once they have voted, you must then determine how much tile is needed for the project and figure the cost to the school district. You will be presenting your research and findings to a panel of school administrators and school board members.

▶ Time travel! You are taking a journey back in time. You work as Thomas Edison's assistant. Using the perspective of that period, write a scientific journal article that probes the problems that you encountered in conceiving and implementing the processes of electric power generation and distribution.

▶ What is the American dream? Has it changed over the generations? Do Americans still seek to live the American dream? Describe your American dream. From this research, analyze and interpret what the American dream is today and how it shapes our American identity.

▶ How has Maya Angelou's poetry shaped modern thinking? Analyze and interpret the poems that you feel have had great social impact and influence.

The Stanford Center for Opportunity Policy in Education (SCOPE) has created a toolkit to assist task designers. Its task development guidelines promote student engagement and include the following dimensions: clear purpose, relevance, authenticity, autonomy, higher-order thinking skills, collaboration, self-assessment, and overarching engagement question. The tool can be found on the center's website.[5]

Assessment as a System

Assessment is a system of student evaluation, not a single action or product. In designing their units, educators need to consider how each assessment item in the unit integrates purposefully and seamlessly with instruction. To see how an assessment task is connected to its competencies, performance indicators, and products of learning, let's unpack the following science task that was described earlier:

Time travel! You are taking a journey back in time. You work as Thomas Edison's assistant. Using the perspective of that period, write a scientific journal article that probes the problems that you encountered in conceiving and implementing the processes of electric power generation and distribution.

The launch of the task invites students to connect with both the competencies and the essential question and standards of the unit. An *essential question* is part of the UbD framework. It is a thought-provoking, open-ended question used to guide thinking throughout a unit. Teachers generally design the essential questions, but students can also design their own essential question in an inquiry-based project of their own design. It is very important that teachers communicate effectively the transparency of the connection between what students are doing and why they are doing it. Once that is established, the topics, content, and skills can then be defined. That is when the research phase begins.

The New Hampshire science competencies addressed in this task include the following:

1. *Systems and system models*: Students will demonstrate the ability to investigate and analyze human designed system in terms of its boundaries, inputs, outputs, interactions, and behaviors and use this information to develop a system model that can be used to understand and empirically and evaluate the accuracy of models in terms of representing the underlying system.

2. *Energy and matter in systems*: Students will demonstrate the ability to analyze evidence from a variety of sources (investigations, models) to predict, connect and/or evaluate the cycling of matter and flow of energy within and between systems to understand, describe, or predict possibilities and limitations of systems.[6]

Unpacking these competencies further into their performance indicators sets the stage for students to research the content. For skills, the teacher would provide learning centers on the appropriate investigation on electricity during the research phase of the work. Performance indicators include the following:

▸ I can investigate and analyze Edison's model for the generation of electric power and its distribution. (DOK level 2: investigation and research on Edison's model; DOK level 3: analyzing the model)

- I can conduct appropriate investigations in electricity safely. (DOK level 2: performing the lab investigation; DOK level 3: analyzing and summarizing lab data results)
- I can evaluate the flow of electrical energy in a system based on Edison's designs. (DOK level 3: interpreting and evaluating the flow of electrical energy in a system)
- Using historical perspective, I can communicate effectively, in writing, the problems in conceiving and designing an electrical energy distribution system. (DOK levels 3 and 4: using historical perspective, evaluating difficulties in conceiving and designing an energy distribution system)
- Additional "I can" statements can be added to further define the DOK levels 1 and 2 learning targets that students may need to learn content and skills or to help the student reach the performance indicators stated previously.

When the research and lab investigation phases of the work are completed, the students then apply what they have learned to the product: the scientific journal article. This piece of writing will be assessed for its scientific content. Because the product is also informational writing, it could be used to address one or more ELA competencies.

To do this work, students will need rubrics to guide the quality of the development of this work: a research rubric, a lab investigation rubric, and a scientific writing rubric customized to the content.

Holistic Proficiency Scales

Because proficiency scales set the stage for rubric design in CBE systems, the rubrics must be comprehensively and intentionally designed. For that reason, I suggest designing a metarubric for proficiency. Teachers can then use and further customize the metarubric when designing specific task rubrics. This work is very important when grading systems are developed. The holistic proficiency rubric should be designed at the system level so that all grading across the district promotes valid and reliable indicators of proficiency.

A holistic proficiency scale is generally designed by a group of teachers and administrators who are developing the CBE grading system as a guidepost for teachers to use in their own rubrics. It guides the language of the set points for proficiency when teachers design their task rubrics. The holistic proficiency scale must describe the performance expectations using DOK language. In the holistic proficiency scale in table 5.1, competency is defined in the language from DOK level 3 actions.

It is much easier to begin this work using a three-point scale—Competent with Distinction, Competent, and Not Yet Competent. We'll discuss the difficulties of converting task rubrics to grading rubrics in chapter 7, but the conversion can be done. Note that the language in the Competent descriptor fits the language of the performance indicator classified at DOK level 3. The research rubric in table 5.2 from the ELO demonstrates how the holistic proficiency metarubric can easily be customized. Take the time to examine how the performance indicators, derived from the competency statements, demonstrate the students' ability to apply their learning, where DOK is declared as a criterion for both the learning targets and the assessment targets.

TABLE 5.1   Metarubric for examining student proficiency

LEVEL DESCRIPTOR	PERFORMANCE INDICATORS
Exemplary (E) or Competent with Distinction (CwD)	▪ Various indicators demonstrate the analysis and synthesis of course content materials within the discipline and/or the extension of conceptual understanding to other disciplines. ▪ Various indicators demonstrate that the student clearly and effectively communicates his or her analytical and critical thinking, abstract reasoning, and problem solving, with precision and accuracy within the content area.
Proficient (P) or Competent (C)	▪ Various indicators demonstrate the application and transfer of essential content and skills. There is sufficient evidence to indicate the student effectively communicates his or her analytical and critical thinking, abstract reasoning, and problem solving with precision and accuracy within the content area.
Insufficient Evidence of Proficiency (INS) or Not Yet Competent (NYC)	▪ There is insufficient evidence to indicate the student can apply and transfer essential course content and skills. There is insufficient evidence to indicate the student effectively communicates his or her analytical, critical, and abstract thinking and problem solving with precision and accuracy within the content area.

TABLE 5.2   Rubric tuned to metarubric for proficiency

COMPETENT WITH DISTINCTION	COMPETENT	NOT YET COMPETENT	
Students evaluate and refine information-gathering strategies to maintain their focus in the energy and matter competency and the systems competencies. The students elaborate on connections between the information gathered, how they refine their learning according to information gathered, and possible alternative directions for their learning.	Students formulate information-gathering strategies to focus learning on energy and matter competency and the systems competencies. The students communicate how they refine their learning according to the information gathered.	Students use an information-gathering strategy that allows them to add to their general body of knowledge. The students communicate the relationship between the information and the direction of their learning.	Students compile information related to the general content of their learning goals.
Students compare and contrast information from a variety of documented sources that represent multiple perspectives related to their learning goals.	Students use information from a variety of documented sources that represent multiple perspectives related to their learning goals.	Students use information from sources representing a single perspective related to their learning goals.	Students use information from a single source.
Students defend the inclusion or exclusion of information according to its relevance to their learning goals, essential question, or both.	Students describe their choices to include or exclude information according to its relevance to their learning goals, essential question, or both.	Students identify information connected to their learning goals, essential question, or both.	
Students defend the validity of information by evaluating the degree of objectivity and the accuracy of sources.	Students analyze the validity of information by investigating the degree of objectivity and the accuracy of sources.	Students gather information while checking the credibility of sources.	Students use information from sources without checking credibility.
Students demonstrate control of and fluency in applicable language, offer a synthesis of the information with their essential question, and defend how they apply this information to accomplishing their task goals.	Students demonstrate a command of applicable language, assess and organize the connections they have found between the information and their essential question, and describe how they apply this information to their task goals.	Students use applicable terms or concepts. The students describe connections they have found between the information, their essential question, and their task goals.	Students use applicable terms or concepts.

Guidelines for designing high-quality rubrics have been established by many authors. Kay Burke clearly distinguishes when to use rubrics and when to use checklists.[7] The use of student checklists for completion criteria such as steps in a writing process or product completion are powerful tools for both students and teachers. For students, the checklists give them the opportunity to self-reflect on their progress to date, and for teachers, the checklists allow teachers to know where students are in their daily work. Erika Stofanak, a CBE specialist, made extensive use of these checklists when teaching world language. She would have her students use index cards placed at the corner of their desks to record their work. She collected these formative assessment checks daily to learn where her students were in the work. The practice helped her shape instruction for the following day.

Unlike checklists, rubrics should be connected to the performance criteria based on the competencies. To guide rubric design, I have adapted the work of Lisa Almeida and Larry Ainsworth to the design criteria for CBE rubrics.[8]

To design a CBE rubric that describes achievement levels for proficiency, begin first with the descriptor for Competent using language drawn from DOK level 3: various indicators demonstrate the application and transfer of essential content and skills. There is sufficient evidence to indicate the student effectively communicates his or her analytical and critical thinking, abstract reasoning, and problem solving with precision and accuracy within the content area.

To meet the criteria for Competent with Distinction, the student would have to meet all the criteria for Competent and would stretch into the performance criteria of level 4: various indicators demonstrate the analysis and synthesis of course content materials within the discipline or the extension of conceptual understandings to other disciplines, or both.

Not Yet Competent moves to the other side of Competent in its descriptors. In a general sense, Not Yet Competent students may inconsistently demonstrate the Competent criteria, incorrectly demonstrate the criteria, or cannot transfer or apply their knowledge in the context of the task: There is insufficient evidence that the student can apply and transfer essential course content and skills. There is also insufficient evidence that the student effectively communicates analytical, critical, and other forms of abstract thinking and problem solving with precision and accuracy within the content area.

One distinction made in assessments is that work cannot be assessed if it is not turned in or seen by the teacher. Therefore, teachers cannot use task rubrics to assess students who do not submit work. These students fall into a different category: Insufficient Work Shown, or IWS. Because of the lack of evidence, proficiency against competency cannot be determined. Ideally, in a CBE environment, this situation is dealt with in a timely fashion at the time of the learning and not at the end of the unit or term.

Validation and Calibration

Tasks need not be designed by individual teachers. The validation of a performance task can be a very powerful learning experience for teachers and can provide job-embedded professional development. Consider task validation as a quality-control measure to ensure the highest quality in both the learning experience and the assessment measures. The aforementioned task development guidelines prepared by the Stanford Center for Opportunity Policy in Education are an excellent tool for giving educators the feedback they need to refine a task before launching it.

Beyond this type of task validation, professional learning communities can also calibrate the rubrics used in the task, to improve the quality of the rubrics. The only way to improve a rubric is to use it and then study how it was used in scoring student work. Rhode Island Department of Education and the National Center for the Improvement of Educational Assessment offer an excellent calibration protocol for use by professional learning communities.[9]

This calibration protocol calls for members of the group to use the following process:

1. Examine the task prompt, rubric, and score sheet.
2. Ask clarifying question of the task author.
3. Read and score samples of student work individually.
4. Share scores.
5. Discuss differences in scores, justify scores, and resolve scoring issues by suggesting changes to the task prompt or rubric.

It may be helpful in this process to provide a full set of teacher and student directions in addition to the task prompt or description. Sometimes the cause for

[handwritten margin note: Rubric as living document]

scoring discrepancies may lie in the directions that were given to a student as part of the task launch.

The unit template used in CBE can easily be expanded to project-based learning, ELOs, and capstone projects. The unit template described in chapter 3 (figure 3.1) can now be expanded to include the assessment plan (figure 5.2).

DEEPER LEARNING OPPORTUNITIES

Beyond performance tasks embedded in units of instruction, three types of competency-based learning opportunities for students can significantly deepen their learning. Project-based learning, ELOs, and capstone experiences allow students longer learning time for tackling a complex problem or project in ways that multiple competencies can be addressed and assessed.

Project-Based Learning

Traditionally, projects are used as culminating events in units. I generally tell teachers that if they are getting back twenty-four of the same products, it is time to rethink their project design!

Nationally, we are very fortunate to have the Buck Institute for Education (www.bie.org) at the forefront of leadership in project-based learning. Buck Institute's planning templates and project management resources provide teachers with excellent tools to embed project-based learning as the main highway for learning. In project-based learning, the project *is* the learning. Students don't learn first and then do a project. Instead, they are hooked into the project and then step back into the content and skills acquisition they need to apply what they have learned to an inquiry they have developed. The institute also houses a database of projects in most curriculum areas at all levels, allowing teachers to begin with a project that they can further customize or to add a new project to the bank for other teachers to use.

Project-based learning provides deep learning because few projects can be siloed into one content area. In addition, the strong ties that these projects typically have to the community and the high degree of student choice and voice in project development and management allows students to engage in personalized learning opportunities. A critical element of this type of learning is the essential question or driving question that signals student inquiry.

FIGURE 5.2 Simplified template for a CBE unit of study, parts 1 and 2: competency statements and assessment

Title of unit: Length of unit:

Teacher:

Course:

Previous unit:

Next unit:

COMPETENCY STATEMENTS		
List course/grade-level competencies:	**Unit competencies** *(Tag each competency to the course/grade-level competencies.)*	
	Essential question(s) *(Should be provocative, having more than one answer.)*	
	Acquisition of content knowledge and skill *(Notate and cite in a full statement for each standard.)*	
(Use the construct: "Students will understand that . . ." or "Students will demonstrate the ability to . . . [depth of knowledge level 3 or 4].")	Students will know . . .	Students will be skilled at . . .

ASSESSMENT		
Evaluative criteria	**Evidence**	
Performance task description:	Performance indicators: "I can" statements:	Depth of knowledge:
Formative tasks and assessments that support learning		
Rubrics *(Attach rubrics and checklists that are used by students.)*		
Performance task validation date:	Members of validation team: Comments:	
Calibration date:	Members of calibration team: Comments:	

Project-based learning essentially is a great fit for learning in CBE. With a well-designed project, many competencies can be addressed across several curriculum areas. Projects by their very nature require exhibition, defense, or publication, and these elements are built into the design of the work.

The challenge in moving toward a project-based learning design is time. Projects take time, and many school schedules make it very hard for students to engage in project work for an extended time. The entire school can try creative scheduling as part of a master schedule or can alter an existing schedule to allow for project time.

We have learned a great deal from schools whose philosophy of learning is project based. High Tech High, a group of eleven public charter schools in San Diego, uses a project-based learning model in its design.[10] Students have quite a bit of autonomy in developing their project idea. Students design the project, tune it, do the work, and exhibit the project in a cycle of work in project-based learning. High Tech High's commitment to deeper learning exemplifies how projects increase the complexity of learning.

In another example, project time is a part of every day at Summit Public Schools (headquarters Redwood City, California). Students become innovators, problem solvers, and creators as they engage in projects that mimic real-world scenarios.[11]

While High Tech High and Summit Public Schools have emerged as national models in project-based learning, many other schools are using this type of learning as their entry points into CBE. Maple Street Magnet School, a public K–5 elementary school in Rochester, New Hampshire, is a well-established school that embraces personalized, project-based learning. Each child in the school has his or her own personal learning plan and engages daily in project-based learning that stresses delivery of mainly the social studies and science curricula. In this school, the literacy and numeracy programs are highly differentiated learning times in the morning, with project time reserved for afternoons. Throughout their time at the school, students engage in projects, many community based, and are grouped by interest, or in grade-level combinations, or in a single grade. Their projects are competency based, drawing from the district competencies, and are further fleshed out by performance indicators. Monique Boudreau and Sarah Bond, teachers at Maple Street, eloquently describe in "Voices from the Field: Project-Based Learning" the contribution that powerful projects have made to their CBE model.

VOICES FROM THE FIELD

PROJECT-BASED LEARNING

By Monique Temple-Boudreau and Sarah Bond,
Maple Street Magnet School, Rochester, New Hampshire

After five years of using project-based learning as an instructional approach, we have learned that the most in-depth learning occurs when we ensure that students' educational experiences reflect their interests and inquiries and are relevant to their lives. As teachers, we begin by outlining what our hopes and dreams are for the project, according to competencies created in our school district. We then use those competencies to promote student agency (i.e., students' autonomy over their learning) and personalized learning.

Last year, we embarked on a multi-age, cross-classroom, collaborative journey in our project-based work to investigate colony collapse disorder occurring in bee colonies, a topic that stemmed from our schoolwide focus on sustainability. We believed that this topic would be meaningful to our students, in light of their prior experiences. We looked at the big picture, decided on our essential question, and referred to our present knowledge: What is happening to the bees? Why is this problem significant? What can we do to help? Next, we began to gather resources and invite other staff members to join us in this project. Collaborating on the project required a great deal of time, dedication, and flexibility as we planned valuable experiences and created a rubric that would allow both kindergarteners and first-graders to demonstrate competency. Creating the rubric was the most challenging aspect of the project. We found ourselves simultaneously beginning another more complex and necessary journey: the development of multi-age learning progressions that would enhance the efficacy of our existing competency-based model.

Kindergarteners and first-graders spent six weeks learning about what is happening to the bees. As teachers, we learned alongside our students, acting as facilitators. In this role, we had to adapt our plans according to student responses to a variety of hands-on experiences, discussions, videos, literature, and visits from local experts, including a beekeeper and a horticultural specialist. These experiences directly informed our guiding questions and allowed students to gain a deeper understanding of the importance of bees in relation to people's food. Throughout this work, students collaborated with their families, conducted research at home, and were independently motivated to share that knowledge with their peers. This interaction resulted in students' ability to serve as experts themselves about the parts of plants, pollination, and most importantly, colony collapse disorder.

The students could choose the outcome of their learning, how they would share what they had learned—the significance of colony collapse—and how to educate others about what they could do to help save the bees. Students brainstormed ideas about who their audience would be, along with various modes of communication, before selecting how they would effectively communicate their message to an authentic, public audience in our city of Rochester, New Hampshire. Final projects included creating posters with both traditional tools and modern technology, such as applications like Book Creator and Keynote. Other modes of sharing their message included creating movies, newscasts, social media platforms, interviewing experts, and writing persuasive letters. The students were so vested in this topic that their targeted audiences included the president of the United States, the mayor, and local farmers. The public presentation of these final projects enabled students to demonstrate a sense of ownership and pride in their learning as well as an opportunity to be an active, contributing member of our local community.

At the conclusion of our project, our most significant reflection as educators was the realization that we had missed key opportunities to document student learning along the way. We underemphasized how significant the video and photo documentation, anecdotal records, and recorded children's dialogue was in demonstrating student knowledge and competency in a developmentally appropriate way. The value and DOK within personalized learning and a project-based approach is heavily embedded within the process. As we move forward with our project work, our goal is to continuously highlight this documentation and its value, making it more visible to all audiences. By allowing our guiding question to evolve organically and by participating in the learning alongside our students, we emphasize the journey itself. More importantly, we enable our students to achieve a DOK that would otherwise be unattainable as we empower our students to be not only successful twenty-first-century learners, but also contributors to our society.

High Tech High, Summit Public Schools, Maple Street Magnet School, and Next Charter School (chapter 3) are but a few models exemplifying the commitment to deeper learning by committing, time, resources, and community outreach so that students can engage in complex learning in a personalized fashion.

Extended Learning Opportunities

In New Hampshire, ELOs were introduced in the state's 2005 Minimum Standards for School Approval. By state policy, every district in the state had to have a local policy that enables students to earn credit for competency-based ELOs in the community. This rule alone challenged the notion that the Carnegie unit is the sole criterion for the granting of high school credit.

The purpose of an ELO is to engage a student in a learning opportunity based on an area of high interest. The student is then connected to a community business or another organization to begin designing the experience. Many New Hampshire high schools have ELO coordinators who match the student's interest to the community organization. Currently, there is a statewide network of ELO coordinators who share their resources and provide support to each other in their program development.

New Hampshire was fortunate to receive a grant from the Nellie Mae Education Foundation in a three-year initiative. Supporting Student Success through Extended Learning Opportunities is helping develop ELO programs in a number of high school sites. Partners in this work included the New Hampshire Department of Education, Plus Time New Hampshire, Kim Carter of the QED Foundation, and Joe DiMartino of the Center for Secondary School Redesign. Additionally, Rob Lukasiak, Kenneth Greenbaum, Charles Gaides, and I represented the Capital Area Center for Education Support.

We learned a great deal from this project as approximately twelve hundred ELOs were completed by 2011, according to the New Hampshire Department of Education in the final project evaluation. In this project evaluation, the University of Massachusetts Donahue Institute noted that when ELOs are designed well, they are characterized by "high expectations, rigor, and learning that is relevant to student goals."[12] The four components that drive the rich learning and rigor in an ELO are research, reflection, product, and presentation; these components drive the ELO competencies by meeting the learning and assessment targets in the ELO. Many schools use rubrics for each of these components to guide students and teachers in the development of the ELO as well as its assessment. Mariane Gfroerer of the New Hampshire Department of Education provides guidelines for ELO design and discusses these four components of a good

ELO.[13] Her work and the statewide policies and resources are available at the department's website.[14] And "Voices from the Field: Assessing Student Learning in Extended Learning Opportunities," by Bonnie Robinson (the curriculum, instruction, and assessment director of Lebanon High School and a leader in the statewide ELO coordinator network), describes how rubrics can help address these four components of ELOs.

VOICES FROM THE FIELD
ASSESSING STUDENT LEARNING
IN EXTENDED LEARNING OPPORTUNITIES

By Bonnie Robinson, EdD, Director of Curriculum, Instruction, and Assessment, Lebanon High School, Lebanon, New Hampshire

Rubrics serve two main functions. First, before an ELO, they give hints about the process and they frame the expectations for students, teachers, and community partners. It is always a good idea to clarify expectations as specifically as possible in the beginning, and the rubrics help set the stage for success. Second, at the end of the ELO, the rubrics are useful in assessing student achievement.

Whether students are doing independent studies, internships, performing groups, community service, or any other type of ELO, the four pillars of research, reflection, product, and presentation provide the means by which students will show their learning. The culminating presentation is an oral and visual sharing of all aspects of the ELO and usually includes several members of the ELO team including the teacher, parent, and community partner as well as any individuals the student chooses to invite.

In assessing students' achievement, the four rubrics on research, reflection, product, and presentation have proven to be adaptable for a diverse variety of ELOs. They bring a unifying function to ELOs and help all to understand that there are high academic expectations associated with student work. Students delve deeply into a topic of personal interest or need, and in doing so, they achieve rigorous criteria, meet standards, and master competencies.

Robinson uses the rubrics in tables 5.3 through 5.6 to assess student work in ELOs.[15] Each rubric addresses one of the four components of ELO.

TABLE 5.3   Extended learning opportunities (ELOs), research rubric

EXEMPLARY	PROFICIENT	PROGRESSING	BEGINNING
Students evaluate and refine information-gathering strategies to maintain their focus on targeted competencies. The students elaborate on connections between the information gathered, how they refine their learning according to information gathered, and possible alternate directions for their learning.	Students formulate information-gathering strategies to focus learning on targeted competencies. The students communicate how they refine their learning according to the information gathered.	Students use an information-gathering strategy that allows them to add to their general body of knowledge. The students communicate the relationship between the information and the direction of their learning.	Students compile information related to the general content of their learning goals.
Students compare and contrast information from a variety of documented sources that represent multiple perspectives related to their learning goals.	Students use information from a variety of documented sources that represent multiple perspectives related to their learning goals.	Students use information from sources representing a single perspective related to their learning goals.	Students use information from a single source.
Students defend the inclusion or exclusion of information according to its relevance to their learning goals, essential question, or both.	Students describe their choices to include or exclude information according to its relevance to their learning goals, essential question, or both.	Students identify information connected to their learning goal, essential question, or both.	Students use information in their ELO.
Students defend the validity of information by evaluating the degree of objectivity and accuracy of sources.	Students analyze the validity of information by investigating the degree of objectivity and accuracy of sources.	Students gather information while checking credibility of sources.	Students use information from sources without checking credibility.
Students demonstrate control of, and fluency in, applicable language; offer a synthesis of the information with their essential question; and defend how they apply this information to accomplishing their learning or project goals.	Students demonstrate a command of applicable language, assess and organize the connections they have found between the information and their essential question, and describe how they apply this information to their learning or project goals.	Students use applicable terms or ideas. The students describe connections they have found between the information, their essential question, and their learning or project goals.	Students use applicable terms or ideas.

Source: Modified from Lebanon High School, "ELO Rubrics," accessed March 27, 2017, https://sites.google.com/a/sau88 .net/lhs_elo/elo-rubrics.

TABLE 5.4   Extended learning opportunities, reflection rubric

EXEMPLARY	PROFICIENT	PROGRESSING	BEGINNING
Students identify, evaluate, and revise their short-term goals as needed and justify changes made along the way, explaining how this leads to successfully meeting their long-term goals.	Students identify short- and long-term goals, adjust them as necessary, and determine tasks and next steps in achieving their goals.	Students identify short- and long-term goals and use them to determine tasks and next steps.	Students identify short- or long-term goals.
Students communicate about and analyze the connections between experiences and targeted competencies and predict future behaviors/decisions in light of their analysis ("Next time, . . .").	Students communicate about and analyze the connections between specific experiences and targeted competencies.	Students communicate about experiences and makes a connection to targeted competencies.	Students communicate about experiences, but connections to targeted competencies are not made.
Students describe and analyze problems, assess solutions for the problems, identify a chosen solution for a specific problem, and evaluate the effectiveness of their choice.	Students describe and analyze problems(s), state solutions, and assess solutions for the problem(s).	Students describe problem(s) and state possible solutions(s).	Students identify problem(s).
Students analyze their own growth by making connections between personal ideas and their learning experiences, leading them to new perspectives or insights.	Students analyze their own growth by making connections between personal ideas and their learning experiences.	Students make connections between a personal idea and an experience to establish the basis of a reflection.	Students summarize personal experiences.
Students demonstrate control of media-appropriate language, including vocabulary, syntax, and grammar within an organized structure. Students make few, if any, errors. Intention of thought is clearly communicated.	Students demonstrate control of media-appropriate language, including vocabulary, syntax, and grammar within an organized structure. Errors do not interfere with communication.	Students demonstrate inconsistent control of media-appropriate language, including vocabulary, syntax, and grammar. Organization of the reflection's structure may or may not be evident. Errors detract from communication.	Students demonstrate a lack of control over media-appropriate language, including vocabulary, syntax, and grammar. Students do not reflect in an organized way. Errors disrupt the flow of communication.

Source: Modified from Lebanon High School, "ELO Rubrics," accessed March 27, 2017, https://sites.google.com/a/sau88.net/lhs_elo/elo-rubrics.

TABLE 5.5 Extended learning opportunities, product rubric

EXEMPLARY	PROFICIENT	PROGRESSING	BEGINNING
The product illustrates discovery of complexity or connectivity of the targeted competencies.	The product independently illustrates relevant connections to all the targeted goals and competencies.	The product demonstrates connections to the targeted goals and competencies, dependent on further explanation.	The product is completed with little, if any, evidence of the targeted goals and competencies.
The product meets all the design criteria established by the mentor, certified school personnel, and student in the plan and reflects modifications made in response to authentic feedback.	The product meets all the design criteria established by the mentor, certified school personnel, and student in the plan.	The product meets half the design criteria established by the mentor, certified school personnel, and student in the plan.	The product has little, if any, evidence of meeting the design criteria established by the mentor, certified school personnel, and student in the plan.
The product has been evaluated by the mentor or certified school personnel and an authentic audience. Modifications have been based on feedback or expert critique and/or the product has been adopted for use by the authentic user or audience.	The product has been evaluated by the mentor or certified school personnel and an authentic audience within an appropriate environment. Feedback has been collected.	The product has been shared with the mentor or certified school personnel in an authentic user/audience within an appropriate context. Possible sources of feedback are identified.	The product has been shared with the mentor or certified school personnel for evaluation.
The product reflects a fusion of student interest with the needs of the user or audience. The product is recognized by the mentor or certified school personnel as a unique and original solution to the design criteria and is adopted for use.	The product reflects a fusion of student interest with the needs of the user/audience. The product is recognizes by the mentor or certified school personnel as a unique and original solution to the design criteria.	The product shows evidence of a design based either on the needs of an authentic user/audience or the interest of the student. The product is recognized by the mentor or certified school personnel as an uncommon but successful solution to the design criteria.	The product was external to student interest, or the needs of the user/audience, or both. (Product is the result of an assignment.)
The student creates a collection of artifacts, including those used during the creation of the product and those that describe the process of creation. The artifacts clearly represent authentic feedback. Student's intentional selection of artifacts illustrates key learning breakthroughs.	The student creates a collection of artifacts that were used during the creation of the product or that describe the process of creation. The collection includes clear representation of feedback.	The student creates a collection with appropriate student-created documentation that was used during the creation of the product or that describes the process of creation.	The student creates a collection of artifacts and/or information used in creating the product.

Source: Modified from Lebanon High School, "ELO Rubrics," accessed March 27, 2017, https://sites.google.com/a/sau88.net/lhs_elo/elo-rubrics.

TABLE 5.6 Extended learning opportunities, presentation rubric

EXEMPLARY	PROFICIENT	PROGRESSING	BEGINNING
The presentation communicates the information seamlessly through logical organization; introduction of, and clear focus on, the topic; smooth transitions; well-chosen supporting details; and a coherent conclusion. The student's delivery uses a variety of strategies to engage the audience, and the student responds to audience cues.	The presentation communicates the information through logical organization and clear focus. The student's delivery is appropriate to the audience, context, and purpose.	The presentation communicates the information despite inconsistent organization and/or delivery.	The presentation does not communicate intended information, because organization, delivery, or both interfere.
The student frequently integrates relevant supporting materials that add or clarify information for the presentation.	The student integrates relevant supporting materials that add or clarify information for the presentation.	The student infrequently references supporting materials, which may or may not add information to the presentation.	The student has materials that interfere with the presentation or are not referenced.
The student explains the reasons for choosing the goals of the learning experience, communicates how the student used the learning experience to address the targeted competencies, and makes further connections to prior and future learning.	The student explains the reasons for choosing the goals of the learning experience and how the student used the learning experience to address the targeted competencies.	The student explains the reasons for choosing the goals of the learning experience or the targeted competencies.	The student identifies the goals of the learning experience or the targeted competencies.
The student presents his or her response to the essential question and explains how the response was used to generate additional questions, extensions, or cross-curricular relationships.	The student presents his or her response to the essential question and describes how it guided the work and whether the question changed.	The student states his or her essential question but is unable to articulate how it guided the work.	The student makes no reference to the essential question.
The student selects and presents examples of how his or her research, reflection, and product are interconnected and describes how each element influenced the student's learning along the way.	The student provides examples of how his or her research, reflection, and product illustrate the student's progress toward his or her goals.	The student provides examples of two of the three process components in describing his or her progress toward the learning goals.	The student provides examples of one of the three process components in describing his or her learning goals.
The student communicates what was learned through the successes and challenges of the learning experience and how he or she grew as a result of it.	The student communicates what was learned through the successes and challenges of the learning experience.	The student identifies a success and a challenge of the learning experience, with few details or commentary.	The student identifies a success or challenge of the learning experience without providing any details.

Source: Modified from Lebanon High School, "ELO Rubrics," accessed March 27, 2017, https://sites.google.com/a/sau88.net/lhs_elo/elo-rubrics.

The highly qualified teacher on the ELO teams works with the student to identify the competencies being addressed in the experience. Evidence of the student's learning is collected over time in the four areas, guided by the rubrics, and becomes part of the student's exhibition and defense of their learning to gain credit. As much as the ELO is an academic experience, it also calls into play the personal success skills. As the reflection rubric describes, students can think about any factors that promote or hinder success. Some students may struggle with their ability to self-direct, for example, having trouble with dressing appropriately for the workplace or being on time. Others may have a hard time communicating effectively with adults in the work setting. Students' awareness of their strengths and weaknesses emerge as they reflect often on their experiences.

ELOs are an important part of the tapestry of learning as part of the high school experience. These experiences can be a rich part of a student's personal learning plan in ultimately meeting graduation competencies. Examples of unique ELOs abound. One student gained a geometry credit while working with a stained-glass artisan. Another student earned a physics credit for designing an arcade game. Yet another student earned English credit for writing, producing, and directing a one-act play. ELOs allow students to learn experientially while holding them to high-quality performance standards. An ELO may take several weeks or several months to complete—it is all part of the plan that is supervised by the ELO coordinator.

Learning can happen anywhere and anytime. We no longer need to refer to the classroom as the only learning space. As educators, we can design learning opportunities in a variety of learning environments—in the classroom, online, or in the community.

As you can see, an ELO is more complex than project-based learning. To take this complexity further, consider the capstone experience.

The Capstone Experience

Many traditional and CBE high schools use the capstone experience as an exhibition opportunity at the end of the students' senior year. These are sometimes called senior projects, senior theses, or senior exhibitions. As the word implies, a capstone in our architecture for learning should be the final stone put in place once the building is built.

In a competency-based learning environment, this capstone experience may develop throughout a student's high school years. The capstone is meant to be an independent research project that students engages in for the purpose of presenting their findings and defending their thesis before an evaluation team. Some high schools offer a half-year course for the experience so that students have access to support and advice while working on their capstone project. Some high schools have very high stakes for this capstone experience, in that graduation from high school depends on a successful presentation of learning. We can't expect students to have the ability to perform well with their capstone experience if they have not had the opportunity to build on the academic and personal success skills leading up to the final exhibition. For that reason, educators should provide opportunities for students to exhibit their learning at elementary and middle levels and then again halfway through the high school experience.

In CBE, the capstone experience before graduation allows the students to engage in their area of interest while they develop an inquiry-based project. Because their education is competency based, the students may acquire several credits in different disciplines, depending on the scope and content of their capstone inquiry. The development of the capstone requires frequent conferences with an advisor. Since the lead-up to the capstone may happen over several semesters, it is important for a student to maintain the same advisor. In schools having advisories, this is one function of the advisor—to follow the advisees over several years, supporting them through their capstone experiences.

Within the CBE framework, it has been difficult to isolate performance assessment from instruction. The biggest shift in CBE, in fact, is instructional practice. Ignacio Estrada, a director at the Gordon and Betty Moore Foundation, captured this shift aptly: "If a child can't learn the way we teach, maybe we should teach the way they learn." If we teach so that children may learn, then the focus of our schools will shift from teacher-centered instruction to learner-centered opportunities to learn in many ways, in many places, and at a pace that is set by meeting competency-based performance criteria.

Chapter 6

Learning Pathways

A CORE BELIEF of competency-based education is the recognition that students learn in many ways. The one-size-fits-all learning in traditional classrooms does not provide the varied learning opportunities to support the individual learning needs of each student. The fixed nature of curriculum and instruction is a barrier to the personal learning needs of each learner. CBE turns this paradigm on its head, as figure 6.1 illustrates. Instead of a fixed curriculum driving learning, learning is supported by a flexible curriculum—a personalized pathway that can include in-school and out-of-school options as well as technology-enabled options like

FIGURE 6.1 Comparison of traditional and competency-based learning pathways

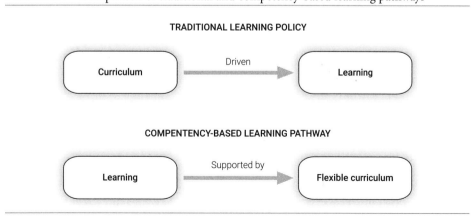

blended and online learning, which enables students to truly move on when they are ready.

A flexible curriculum means that the curriculum adapts with and for the student. A traditional curriculum, spelled out in units of time and owned by the teacher, is inflexible. In the flexible curriculum of CBE, the students move through academic learning progressions according to their demonstrated proficiency. Sometimes, students need longer to learn to proficiency, and other times, the students may already be able to perform to proficiency, with very little time spent on the topic. A flexible, competency-based curriculum also allows students to go deeper into a focus area of curriculum if they show a particular interest. These students would simply spend more time on that topic before moving on. A flexible, competency-based curriculum adapts to the student. The personal learning plan is a management tool for the teacher and a learning tool for the student. It begins in kindergarten and grows with the student through the many learning experiences the child encounters on the pathway to graduation.

At this point in any conversation about CBE with teachers and administrators, many teachers can't quite grasp how they can deliver their curriculum in an adaptable fashion for students. This difficulty is one barrier in thinking through the transformation to CBE. To begin with, there must be a well-structured curriculum in place. A well-written, sequential curriculum with fully developed units of instruction can be very helpful in transitions to a flexible curriculum. In developing learning pathways, educators need to decide how the curriculum will be delivered to the student. At the same time, personal success skills must also be part of the curriculum framework. These skills are generally left out of traditional academic curriculum structures.

An adaptable curriculum that supports individual learning pathways is best designed with the support of technology, because of the need to offer students many ways of learning as well as for management purposes. This use of technology is the breakthrough needed to truly personalize learning for students. It represents one of the most difficult changes to make when schools are moving toward CBE.

Within the traditional framework in education, instruction has been the center of learning, putting it squarely on the shoulders of teachers to own *what* is taught, *when* it is taught, and *when it is assessed and graded.* This teacher-centric approach to learning has deep roots and has resulted in curriculum-driven learning.

Curriculum-driven, teacher-delivered learning fits the face-to-face classroom. Most districts work very hard to develop a K–12 curriculum that is articulated from grade to grade. In this model, each grade level has well-developed units of study that outline the units' content, skills, and assessments. Some curriculum frameworks go as far as planning daily lessons, which teachers are expected to follow and on which their professional performance evaluations are drawn. In some districts, delivery of lessons is tightly scheduled in curriculum and pacing guides.

Many districts have weak curriculum development, as described previously, because they use a purchased program organized by standards-aligned units. When I ask teachers if I could view their curriculum, I often just receive a copy of the program's teacher resource book and am told that it is their curriculum. The use of purchased programs is more prevalent in grades K–6.

There are advantages and disadvantages to such programs. They help teachers who are new to a school or grade level understand what constitutes the year's teaching units. Standardized programs also provide a level of curriculum delivery, organization, and pacing that ensures learning experiences and assessments across a grade level. The programs also align their curricula with Common Core State Standards or other standards, and the teacher resource book offers detailed lesson planning to guide curriculum delivery. Although the programs tend to be a one-size-fits-all resource, they generally provide options and resources for the teacher to differentiate the curriculum for different groups of students. Some programs also have online resources to supplement the text materials; the supplements may include a text and workbook combination for the student. Because many districts invest thousands of dollars in the multigrade programs and professional development and training for teachers to use the programs, districts often require a high degree of fidelity to the programs. Teachers are not allowed to supplement the curriculum in any way, outside of the programs' own supplements. The district imposes these restrictions because it will generally generate a lot of data over time on the effectiveness of the program in improving student learning.

For the very reasons that purchased curriculum programs are advantageous, they can also be disadvantageous. Strictly paced curriculum delivery can leave some learners in the dust. In spite of a teacher's best effort to teach all the students all the material in the chapter or unit, some students struggle to learn and are moved on to the next unit or chapter anyway. The programs may lack any type of preassessment of the learning goals to determine if students already know the material. Moreover, the purchased programs may not provide a parallel curriculum for those students as part of the curricular materials.

When teachers are pressured by time constraints for curriculum delivery, they may not have the time to be at their creative best. Departing from the curriculum materials for a project or a performance task may not be easy. A major disadvantage of curriculum programs is that professional development within a content area may be stifled. Districts limit their content professional development to additional training in the purchased curriculum instead of broader themes of pedagogy and assessment that may benefit teacher development.

In curriculum-driven, teacher-centric teaching and learning, a student may develop a Swiss cheese learning map. Although the curriculum may be sequential and aligned, the student's learning may not be so well organized and may have gaps. Unlike past generations, today's students move into and out of schools, entering a new school without having the benefit of engagement with that sequential and aligned curriculum that their new district has in place.

My experience as the principal of a middle school for grades 5–8 is illustrative. To fill in some time before an assembly one day, I surveyed a group of eighth-graders at my school. At that time, the district had two K–4 elementary schools in the town. The middle school then brought in students from two surrounding towns for grades 7–8, with a class size of 350 for each of those upper-grades levels. I asked the eighth-graders how many of them have been in the school system for eight years. I was surprised to find that only about 80 percent had started and finished in the same school system. Although we were fortunate to have a common curriculum across all feeder schools in the district, only 80 percent of the students were actually engaged with it for the eight years. Add to that the unlearned curriculum through those eight years, and I now have a greater appreciation for the effect of Swiss cheese learning.

As we will see, personalization does not mean that every student has an electronic device at his or her disposal in school. Personalization means that each student's unique learning pathway is supported, and time is not a barrier. Learning that brings each student to competency is the goal.

PERSONALIZATION

Personalization realizes the shift from teacher-centered to student-centered learning. Barbara Bray and Kathleen McClaskey, leading national experts in personalization, have developed a chart that best explains the differences between personalization, differentiation, and individualization (table 6.1).

Personalization brings the learner into day-to-day decisions about learning. Students have a voice in these decisions, in how they wish to learn something, and in the product of their learning and their agency—the level of control or autonomy they have in their learning. Differentiation is a strategy that teachers use to meet the individual needs of students. All the decisions about student learning are made by the teacher for the students. In differentiation, students are often grouped within a classroom by their ability or by their interest in meeting these needs. Individualization is a form of customization for the purpose of meeting the student's individual needs, but the choice, voice, and agency in directing learning remains with the teacher. To summarize, differentiation and individualization are teacher-led activities, whereas personalization is done by students.

Bray and McClaskey's chart describes in detail the shift in focus from teacher to student, opening up the potential for different learning pathways for students. This detailed chart can be a powerful teacher development tool. By and large, we put a great deal of pressure on our teachers to differentiate instruction. By using this chart in conversations with teachers as part of the development work in moving to CBE, teachers can more easily see the difference. Conversations can shift from the what to the how, given this greater clarity of understanding.

One misconception about implementing student-centered learning is that every student is on an *individual* learning plan. With this notion, teachers think that each student is on a plan specifically written by the teacher for the student, much like an individual education plan for a special-needs student. It is really important to disabuse teachers of this misconception early on when you introduce *personal* learning plans. With extensive discussions about shifting learning to student-centeredness, teachers need to think about what exactly supports

TABLE 6.1 A comparison, differentiation, and individualization as learning pathways

PERSONALIZATION	DIFFERENTIATION	INDIVIDUALIZATION
Learners . . .	The teacher . . .	The teacher . . .
drive their own learning.	provides instruction to groups of learners.	provides instruction to an individual learner.
connect learning with interests, talents, passions, and aspirations.	adjusts learning needs for groups of learners.	accomodates the learning needs for the individual learner.
actively participate in the design of their learning.	designs instruction according to the learning needs of different groups of learners.	customizes instruction according to the learning needs of the individual learner.
own and are responsible for their learning that includes their voice and choice on how and what they learn.	is responsible for a variety of instruction styles for different groups of learners.	is responsible for modifying instruction according to the needs of the individual learner.
indentify goals for their learning plan and benchmarks as they progress along their learning path with guidance from the teacher.	identifies the same objective for different groups of learners as he or she does for the whole class.	identifies the same objectives for all learners with specific objectives for individuals who receive one-on-one support.
acquire the skills to select and use the appropriate technology and resources to support and enhance their learning.	selects technology and resources to support the learning needs of different groups of learners.	selects technology and resources to support the learning needs of the individual learner.
build a network of peers, experts, and teachers to guide and support their learning.	supports groups of learners who are reliant on the teacher for their learning.	understands that the individual learner is dependent on the teacher to support their learning.
demonstrate mastery of content in a competency-based system.	monitors learning using Carnegie unit (seat time) and grade level.	monitors learning according to unit (seat time) and grade level.
become self-directed, expert learners who moinitor progress and reflect on learning based on mastery of content and skills.	uses data and assessments to modify instruction for groups of learners, and provides feedback to individual learners to advance learning.	uses data and assessments to measure progress of what the individual learner learned and did not learn to decide next steps in their learning.

Source: Modified from Barbara A. Bray, and Kathleen A. McClaskey, *Make Learning Personal: The What, Who, Wow, Where, and Why* (Thousand Oaks, CA: Corwin Press, 2014). Reprinted with the authors' permission.

personalized learning. For example, in personalization, the student acquires skills to select and use technology, whereas in differentiation, the technology is chosen for a group of students. Note that there isn't a difference in the actual curriculum, but there is a difference in how students are supported as they move through the curriculum. In using Bray and McClaskey's chart as a self-assessment of current educator skill sets and knowledge, schools can customize professional development to better meet the needs of teachers as they design personalized learning approaches.

When teachers see the shift to student-centered approaches, they are better able to see how technology can be used in supporting individual student learning. A learner's personal learning plan is a key piece to successfully developing personalized learning. It grows with the student, ideally from kindergarten through high school graduation, and allows students to self-reflect and share their thoughts on their learning. In a personal learning plan, the student can create academic, social, and personal goals throughout his or her learning journey from kindergarten to high school graduation. The plan also allows learners to look through the lens of their personal success skills and honestly evaluate how they address those skills. Besides being a rich source of academic goal setting, personal learning plans encourage student reflection on how learning goals have been met relative to the proficiency benchmarks embedded within the curriculum. Important to the personal learning plan's development is the understanding that the student uses the plan both in and out of school. The personal learning plan thus brings the total compass of learning into the process of metacognition and uncovers quite a bit for the child's learning team.

I am reminded of a long walk I took with one of my eighth-grade students when we were on a class trip to Washington, DC, and the surrounding area. On our visit to Gettysburg, I paired off with Dan to see the sights. I had never known that he had such a great interest in the Civil War. He was so excited about sharing much of what he knew as he started making connections to the fields where the battles were fought. That experience often comes back to me. If we had only known that he was such an expert, we could have amplified his experience before, during, and after the visit by having him share and teach his teachers and peers. If Dan had had a personal learning plan, perhaps his interest would have been known, would have grown, and would have been shared even though that interest and expertise was generated on his own, outside school walls. He would have described his interest and passion for US history and recorded the books he had read and the places he had visited. Sharing his personal learning plan with his teachers from an early age would have honored this learning.

If personal learning plans are developed by the learners in school and out of school throughout the year and over many years, how do students develop and share these plans with multiple people over time? Technology can be the best answer for this dilemma, although you don't need an online resource for integrated K–12 personal learning plans to begin developing such plans with students. For that reason, personal learning plans that are part of learning management systems provide continuous access for student input. The management systems also house the curriculum for the student to access and move through. Let's consider how different learning environments can support customized student learning while empowering learners through agency in their learning.

FACE-TO-FACE LEARNING ENVIRONMENTS

Looking into the future, do you think brick-and-mortar schools will be the center of a child's learning experience? This is a great question to ask different audiences. Most parents who send their children to local brick-and-mortar schools are often unaware of anything else. Parents also see the necessity of the traditional school building at the elementary level for child-rearing purposes yet would like more flexibility against the rigid school-day and school-year expectations of the traditional calendar. Even though online and blended learning have had a strong presence in some of our educational systems for some time, in the traditional setting of our local schools, it is hard to think of our schools in any way but the cohort-based, grade-level progression of kindergarten through twelfth grade.

Schools today have great potential to begin using their resources differently by restructuring their physical resources. We are married to the notion that a child enters a school building, walks down the hall, joins his or her age and grade-level peers, and stays with them all day long. One trajectory toward moving to CBE is to challenge the notion that this single-class setting optimizes learning for each student. We know that students enter that classroom with different assets, skills, and knowledge. Moving a school toward CBE can mean, in the early stages, simply striving to serve the diversity of learners. Do grade levels matter?

In introducing the notion of move-on-when-ready, teachers may be stymied by the idea of their students walking down a hall to learn from someone else at a higher or lower grade level. The social and parental concerns are paramount in considering such a change. Teachers can't get their mind around how a move-on-when-ready concept can be organized and managed, given the complexity of scheduling student support. In addition, some parents are not comfortable with the notion of a very young student sitting side by side with much older students as peers, because their child is advanced in literacy or numeracy.

We can do much more to customize student learning using the face-to-face learning environments of our brick-and-mortar schools today. In breaking through this rigid thinking of the past, we can solve some of the potential problems in staffing and resourcing our schools in the future.

Repurposing Learning Spaces

At the early elementary level, imagine a young child entering the school building already known to the teachers through parent conferencing and a play-based assessment by a team of teachers. Our young student is assigned to a small pod of students who share the same teacher at the beginning of the day, at several points during the day, and at the end of the day. This teacher may stay with this pod of students for several years. From the pod at the beginning of the day, the student moves to the appropriate small-group learning setting that is based on ongoing formative assessments. Our young student may have several teachers work with him or her in those academic groups. These teachers continually update the learning profile that is part of the child's personal learning plan, while the student grows in the ability to interact with this plan as his or her communication skills develop.

As we will see, this type of learning space engenders the use of technology to curate and customize the content. However, if technology isn't available, these face-to-face learning spaces can more easily customize learning than can whole-class instruction in grade-based learning. The nimbleness that a team can use to shift learning spaces for small groups to meet the needs of students is also promoted. Will there ever be whole-class direct instruction in this newer kind of learning environment? Indeed, yes! Direct instruction will continue to be one of many strategies used for small-group instruction. Young learners will always be with their developmentally appropriate peers whenever peer learning is important, whereas they will be flexibly moved to the appropriate learning group within a grade span according to where they are on their learning progressions.

Ideally, a school redesign effort would grow as the students develop. Imagine a student arriving at the door of a middle school, personal learning plan in hand (or online) and having developed both academic and personal success skills in a competency-based learning environment. This young student will need a unique combination of developmental support and school structure to support the child's emerging adolescence.

As debate lingers on whether adolescents should be housed in separate schools in a middle-level grade-span configuration, middle-schoolers still go to school in a variety of groupings: K–8, 5–8, 6–8, 7–8, and even some configurations incorporating ninth grade.

What remains clear is that middle-schoolers are unique. The Association for Middle Level Education's "This We Believe" statement clearly articulates that middle-level students need developmentally appropriate learning environments that are challenging, empowering, and equitable.[1] Sound familiar? In CBE school-redesign efforts, middle schools that use team-based approaches that include flexible scheduling and advisory programs can further customize those practices. In many districts I have worked in, it is often the middle school team that has the fewest barriers to the developmental work. One advantage middle schools have in their transition to CBE lies in the common planning time often built into the school day for interdisciplinary teams. The schools create additional flexibility in the use of time and grouping arrangements in the face-to-face instructional model and then often move to more blended learning strategies as a breakthrough. In elementary and high school settings, scheduling is a more greater challenge than in middle schools.

High schools come in all shapes and sizes. The common structures I have observed include the following:

- traditional high schools with seven or eight fixed instructional periods daily and with ability levels built into the course offerings
- traditional, comprehensive high schools on block scheduling or modified block scheduling, either with or without ability-level course offerings
- traditional, competency-based high schools, some of which may have ability levels built into the course offerings, with in-house smaller learning communities or houses that organize both teachers and students
- nontraditional, course-based high schools offering personalized learning strategies across several learning environments (combinations of on-campus learning, online learning, and community-based learning)
- non-course-based, competency-based, project-based learning high schools

For most of the high school types mentioned above, much about the school structure is fixed and baked into the face-to-face, whole-class model. That does not mean that there are no personalized contexts for learning in these institutions, but personalized learning may not be the norm in the culture for learning.

Some of the most personalized learning environments, some of which are competency-based by design, sometimes fall under the banner of alternative high schools. The term *alternative* may carry with it some misconceptions. For example, when I was staying at a hotel in Westchester County, New York, I happened to pick up a local magazine that had an article showcasing a number of alternative schools in the area. The piece described them as rigorous, highly personalized learning environments focused on the individual needs and achievements of their students. Many students are drawn to these schools from the traditional pressures to succeed found in the regions' other high schools. After reading the article, I was convinced that if the word *alternative* had been removed from the title and the school descriptions, most parents would want their children to attend those high schools not at as alternative schools but simply as the best choice for their children.[2]

In many traditional high schools, blended learning strategies are just beginning to make their way into teaching and learning while online courses may be offered as a separate curricular offering. Elementary, middle, and high school levels of teaching and learning are unique. For the sake of our learners, we must make their K–12 progression make sense. We found this out in New Hampshire when the policies related to competencies applied only to the high school level. Middle school students experienced learning culture shock to encounter a different performance expectation for their learning and a shift in grading practices just by virtue of their walking into school on their first day as high school freshmen. This lack of continuity was the stimulus for the early adopters in New Hampshire to move to K–12 CBE designs. It made sense in supporting the learning pathways for students.

Our goal should be to move current structures and cultures for teaching and learning into designs that personalize learning for each child in the K–12 journey. Although intentions may be genuine, it is difficult to realize this transformation without consideration of the advantages that blended and online learning offers in designing competency-based personalized pathways to college and career readiness.

BLENDED AND VIRTUAL LEARNING ENVIRONMENTS

Personalized learning may or may not be competency based. So too, blended learning environments may or may not be personalized or competency based. In the early development of blended learning models, there was a leap to push the concept that blended learning meant one-to-one computing opportunities and that because a student used his or her own computer, learning was personalized. Let's be clear: meeting the unique needs of learners, whatever it takes, and giving them choice, voice, and agency in their learning are what personalization in learning is all about. In CBE, this personalization means having the student meet defined proficiency before moving forward in their learning.

Michael Horn and Heather Staker, in their authoritative book, *Blended*, define blended learning as (1) a formal program of student learning where the student learns, in part, online and has control over the place, pace, and path of the learning; (2) student learning that takes place in a brick-and-mortar location outside the home and under the supervision of teachers; and (3) the integrated pathway between the online and face-to-face learning opportunities.[3]

With this definition, it can be seen that not all computer use in the classroom constitutes blended learning. I once toured a school that touted itself as a pioneer in blended learning, only to find out that students simply had their own Chromebooks and used them for note taking and turning assignments in digitally. There was no customization of learning for individual students. It appeared to be no more than face-to-face teaching and learning in whole-class teaching while the computers were used with somewhat greater efficiency than pen and notebooks.

The shift for teachers to design learning using technology can be daunting. As technology has developed fairly rapidly, schools are having quite a bit of difficulty keeping up with technological demand. Historically, in the early days of school computing, there never seemed to be enough stand-alone computers and licensed software for all the students to access when it was needed. The cost of the units and the complex networks of servers often limited the true number of units that were affordable to a school. As computing moved to more web-based applications, hardware costs decreased but network demands and bandwidth became problematic and again had a hefty price tag. Access and equity became concerns in schools across the country. Although we still struggle with these issues, technology is becoming easier to acquire and use, especially where students are allowed to bring in their own devices to augment the capabilities of their local schools.

Just as we have both flexible and fixed curricula, teachers and administrators have to decide what approach they want to use in moving toward true personalization. There are many software products that essentially present a fixed curriculum online. The student goes online, moves through the fixed presentation of the materials, and completes the assessment. This isn't the use of technology we imagine when we design blended learning in the competency-based environment. In CBE, students move on when they demonstrate proficiency, and the blended environment supports greater choice and voice in their learning.

Shifting to personalized approaches using technology pushes and stretches the pedagogical strategies of the face-to-face teaching model. Teachers who have moved to these blended strategies have told me that their biggest accommodation has been in giving up total control of teaching and learning. Some people refer to this as the shift in the teacher's role from the sage on the stage to the guide on the side. I prefer to think of the teacher more as an orchestra leader. Today's teachers in a blended learning environment need to understand how groups play or learn together while still learning the skills of music theory and instrumentation individually. The orchestra leader can hear, see, and lead while tapping into an individual's talents and moving the individual to greater proficiency over time.

The goal of blended learning (combining face-to-face and online learning) is best reached by groups of teachers learning by doing. Teachers can make great progress by simply working together and seeking out good professional resources like *Blended*, the Getting Smart website (www.gettingsmart.com), the Education Elements website (www.edelements.com), the Clayton Christensen Institute for Disruptive Innovation's website (www.blendedlearning.org). From teachers' collaborative efforts and knowledge resources, they may either dip their toes into the shallow end of the pool or dive right in and implement. Acquiring new blended learning strategies brings professional learning opportunities from the "train them up" model to a CBE model that teachers will be creating for their students. By investigating new strategies based on research and taking virtual field trips to school models, teachers can collaborate, innovate, and try these new approaches to learning that engages students.

The strategies most commonly seen in true blended learning environments include the station rotation model, the flex model, the à la carte model, and the enriched virtual model. All these strategies have been put forth by Horn and Staker as starting points for teachers to explore to realize the true potential of blended learning.[4]

The station rotation model is similar to the learning center model in traditional learning. In this model, the teacher's station allows a small group of students to tap into the teacher's coaching and expertise. More individualized attention is given during this time. From that station, students learn individually online. Ideally, the online learning resource adapts to where the students are on their personal learning progression and tracks or monitors student progress. If a student experiences difficulty, the software adapts to the learner's needs and toggles more resources to strengthen the foundational learning skills needed for success. Once a station is completed at the student's own pace and, ideally, at his or her choice of place, it is time for the student to model independent learning. In the CBE context, this step would be where the student would be applying his or her learning in a performance task designed with the required orientation to DOK so that the embedded assessment truly measures proficiency.

Summit Public Schools uses a lab rotation model in the pacing of its school day. Students spend a portion of their day learning online, then move to the classroom with a seamless integration between the learning in the two settings. Flexibility in grouping students by responding to the formative assessments in the online learning is essential.

When the term *blended learning* first arrived on our doorsteps, many thought that the flipped classroom was the sole strategy. Khan Academy, Mountain View, California, was a pioneer in taking math education, breaking it down into small topics, providing online teaching and learning opportunities, and monitoring student progress that teachers could access. The idea of the flipped classroom is that the student does online learning independently, sometimes even for homework when possible, while maximizing classroom time for teachers to work with students in small groups or individually. Basically, whatever the teacher would teach in whole-class direct instruction the student would learn independently online, allowing the teacher the time to work more productively with students face-to-face.

In the individual rotation model, students move through their learning using a customized playlist. These playlists can be based on formative assessments and other monitoring of learning. The student goes online and, once logged on, is presented with a playlist of learning activities customized for him or her. There is a growing list of free, online course content that can be used by teachers for this customization. For example, Gooru is a community of practice for educators across the country. Teachers upload lessons on various topics. A teacher need only search the vast database for appropriate lessons and plug them into playlists for individual students.

The flex model relies more heavily on the student's engaging in online learning through course work that is supplemented by face-to-face learning or project-based learning. The flex model sometimes provides the support that students require when they are taking online courses for credit recovery.

The à la carte model simply provides a broader course offering for students who may not be able to take a particular course in school, for a variety of reasons. For example, one small elementary school wanted to offer its students world languages but was unable to find the resources to do so. It was, however, able to offer the space, time, and technology so that students could choose a language to explore online. In small rural high schools, it is often difficult to offer advanced courses or a variety of electives. Offering online courses while giving local support can complement and complete a course of studies.

Virtual learning sometimes means that a student need never step into a brick-and-mortar school—100 percent of learning takes place online, often in a virtual school. The backbone of learning in the enriched virtual model is the online courses that the student takes independently but is supported by face-to-face enrichment time with teachers in a school setting.

Whether you are using the scan codes in *Blended*, researching various models on the websites already mentioned, or consulting the CompetencyWorks website, (www.competencyworks.org) to read case studies, you can see how these various blended models can be designed into opportunities for students to learning deeply and to meet competency in a personalized fashion.

Competency development, rich assessment, and new learning pathways are the hallmark of CBE. They represent the evolution of traditional learning into a new picture of teaching and learning. One aspect of traditional teaching and learning must respond to the changing substructure of teaching and learning in CBE: grading. We'll look at grading in the next chapter.

Chapter 7

Competency-Based Grading

OF ANY AREA OF SCHOOL TRANSFORMATION, grading reform presents itself as the most problematic. There seems to be an assumption that for a school or district to move to CBE, a new grading system must be in place first. Here is some sage, simple advice for anyone thinking that grading reform must be part of the initial work in CBE reform: don't do it! Grading reform simply can't be the engine for this work. Before you make any major shifts in grading, you must tend to the most important tasks in this transformation: developing competency designs, performance assessments, and learning pathways. In fact, changes in grading in support of CBE can take place gradually. Let's examine the implications of moving from traditional grading systems to competency-based grading systems while building a coherent system of communicating learning from kindergarten to twelfth grade.

TRADITIONAL GRADING

Traditional grading is a time-based system. Typically, a school year is divided into four quarters that essentially set the time constraints for reporting. For the most part, the curriculum is planned into these quarters so that assessment schedules line up with the ability of a teacher to render his or her grade reports in time for report generating. To meet this schedule, teachers design their grading criteria and work completion schedules to meet the published deadlines for grade reporting. Most often, a grading program will compute a final grade using the weighting that the teacher places on the grades entered into the information system's grade book.

The typical entry of grades is by format of assessment: test, quiz, homework, project, and so forth.

Traditional grading may vary significantly from district to district or sometimes within a district. For the purposes of anchoring a reference point for traditional grading, many or all of the following characteristics define traditional grading systems:

- the use of a hundred-point grade-reporting system
- the use of an A, B, C, D, and F grade-reporting system
- the entry of grades into grade books by the format of the assessment (e.g., quiz, test, project)
- the inclusion of nonacademic factors such as effort, behavior, and conduct in calculating an average or a grade
- the reporting of only one grade per content area on a report card in a reporting period
- a time-based system of grading (generally quarters or trimesters)
- the calculation of one or more types of honor rolls according to quarter or trimester grades
- the use of averaging to arrive at a final grade for a reporting period
- teacher-to-teacher variability in calculating a grade for a reporting period
- students penalized one or more grade levels for late work
- a grade penalty for reassessment on summative assessments
- grading and averaging of homework as part of a grade for a reporting period
- the use of a zero grade for work that is not completed or not turned in by a student
- weighting of midterm or final examination grades, or both, into an overall course grade
- averaging of quarterly or trimester grades into an end-of-course or end-of-year grade
- makeup work and extra-credit work allowed by teachers in arriving at a grade for a reporting period; no criteria set by school or district for this extra-credit work

- ▶ lack of consistent definition in academic levels if middle or high school uses academic levels in course structure; teacher-to-teacher variability in the content, skills, and performance criteria for academic levels
- ▶ student grades sometimes used as criteria for participation in extra-curricular events or social functions within the school year
- ▶ grade point averages and class ranking calculated for each student in high school

Do you currently use a traditional grading system in your district? You may answer yes as you think about your middle school or high school grading systems. The crucial question in beginning your grading reform is this: How do we currently communicate student learning from kindergarten to twelfth grade? In working with many schools on grading reform, I have found that this question launches a firmly grounded effort. One strategy that helps a district answer this question is for a team of educators and parents to review, survey, and comment on every report card that a district uses, from kindergarten to twelfth grade. Listed below are observations I have made in conducting this activity in various school districts:

- ▶ K–2 reporting stresses developmental benchmarks and reports on academic performance without using numerical or letter-grade equivalents.
- ▶ Early elementary grade reports often report on local standards without averaging into a single grade.
- ▶ Number grading (a 0–100 scale) or letter grading generally begins in grade 3 or 4.
- ▶ Honor rolls are calculated using number and letter grading.
- ▶ There can be different types of scales within a district and levels, especially in elementary schools. For example, one school may use "Developing," "Meets," "Exceeds," and so on, while another school in the same district uses "In progress," "Novice," and "Proficient."
- ▶ Middle schools may use both number and letter grades, and pluses and minuses may be part of both the number and the letter schemata. Effort, motivation, citizenship (or similar attributes) are graded on a four-point scale by each teacher at the end of a quarter or trimester.

- A ten-point scale may be used in middle schools, whereas, in the same district, a seven-point scale is used (i.e., in middle school 90–100 = A; in high school 93–100 = A).
- At the middle school level, a different grading system may be used for unified arts than is used in academic areas. The arts may or may not be used in calculations for honor roll determination.

At the high school level:

- Grading by course and teacher generally includes numbers or letters that may or may not have a plus or minus designation. High school report cards generally include a report on twenty-first-century skills or a similar set of skills. Grades for these skills and for effort and behavior are generally entered by the teacher at the end of every quarter or trimester. One academic grade is generally reported at the end of a quarter or trimester for a course. In some schools, an academic area is broken out into several smaller topical areas, each receiving a grade, which is then averaged into a single course grade.
- The average, or mean, is the most frequent determiner of a quarter or trimester grade.
- Some high schools and middle schools report semester final exams as a percentage of the end-of-course grade. Weight for final exams can be up to 20 percent of an overall course grade.
- At the high school level, class rank and grade point average (GPA) begin to appear on report cards.
- Weighting of courses may or may not be part of the GPA determination.
- Honor rolls are generally computed on academic (arts included) course grades only.
- Senior class salutatorian and valedictorian are generally determined by GPA alone.

Although these lists represent what is included on report cards, some information is notably absent from most report cards:

- ► the purpose of the report card
- ► the criteria for assigning letter or number grades
- ► at the high school level, what defines a course level (honors, standards, Advanced Placement classes, etc.)

When educators and parents review the report cards used in their district, they soon realized how scattered and open to interpretation grade reporting can be. Going further with this exercise, the next question I asked the group is, What role does grading and grade reporting have in communicating to parents how the school is meeting its vision of the graduate? If the school vision represents a tacit understanding between students, parents, and the school, then grades should represent the evidence that students are learning and being assessed and graded on agreed-on criteria for achieving the vision.

The challenge is to get teachers, parents, administrators, and technology support personnel to agree on a fair grading system that makes sense as a student moves through the K–12 system. But such a system can be done, and done well, when a district is developing CBE grading systems.

STANDARDS-BASED GRADING

In standards-based grade reporting, a grade is entered under a standard, and there may be some ability to weight certain entries. The quarters are essentially isolated from one another once the grade report for the quarter is generated. Most often, to generate an end-of-course grade, the four quarterly grades are averaged. If a student learns to proficiency by the end of a quarter or year, it doesn't seem fair or truly representative of student learning to lower the reported grade by work averaged in from the beginning of the year.

The works of Thomas Guskey, Douglas Reeves, Ken O'Connor, Robert Marzano, and Rick Wormeli (see "Additional Resources" at the end of this chapter) have informed many educators in building quality, standards-based grading systems. Reform in this area has been substantial and represents a step toward competency-based grading because it addresses many of the unfair grading practices used in traditional grading systems. Yet, it often stops at the door of the high school.

A K–8 school I worked with spent two years developing a standards-based grading system for the school. It was based on best practices in standards-based grading. Teachers spent two years reading about, researching, and developing their curriculum to begin their grade-reform efforts. As the first quarter of the next school year ended, the teachers set about producing their new report cards. After the report cards arrived home, I received a call from the superintendent asking me to meet with the principal to help with a problem: when the report cards went home, parents had gone into an uproar. The school had moved from a traditional letter or number system to a four-point grading system. The parents simply had no frame of reference for what the new grades meant and had no idea how the new and old grading systems compared. I felt bad for the teachers and the principal when the superintendent mandated that the report cards be called back in and new ones generated using the old grading system. After two years of good professional work in this area, the entire effort was set back. The superintendent asked if I would present a session to parents on standards-based grading to help the matter. The day of the meeting, I wasn't entirely surprised to find out the meeting venue was changed from the library to the gym!

Whether moving to new grading systems for standards-based reform or for CBE, the one area where parents have a vested interest is their child. They want to know how their child is doing in school, academically and otherwise. They simply want the school to communicate this information clearly.

Two general reasons for misunderstanding can occur when a new grading system is instituted. Parents of older children are familiar with the old way of grading and can feel uncomfortable with a new reporting system that doesn't appear related to the old way. They are also concerned that, should there be negative repercussions on their child's academic standing because of the changes, their child's chances for admission to college may be compromised. On the other hand, parents of younger children do not have this attachment to the old grading system, because they are not used to their children's being graded at all. But problems arise when this young student is formally graded in the K–12 continuum, usually in grades 3–4 in most systems. It is confusing for the child who normally got checks, comments, and stickers to begin receiving grades. Parents are shocked when the nongraded feedback that is generally positive becomes a grade that may not sync with how they view a child's academic standing. Bringing parents and guardians into the conversations that shape the development of either a standards-based report card or a competency-based report card would go a long way in alleviating the adults' discomfort with the new system and could even help them better understand CBE.

In assessing districts against the CBE framework to determine their readiness for moving toward CBE, having a district already using standards-based grading is very advantageous. Many schools that use standards-based reporting have already aligned their academic units to standards across grade levels by discipline and use the same scoring district-wide K–12 system when assessing proficiency. The disconnect in these schools may be that there are no common criteria for Proficient in the scale used in grading. In addition, the schools may not be developing reliable performance assessments with high-quality rubrics. However, the fact that many factors that contribute to grade subjectivity in the traditional system are no longer at play in standards-based grading is a great improvement.

Many standards-based grading systems include these characteristics:

- ▶ reporting student achievement in disaggregated fashion by standard
- ▶ academic grade reporting separate from other factors such as effort, motivation, and citizenship
- ▶ grading moving from traditional letter or number systems to a standards-referenced grade (e.g., Not meeting the standard, Meeting the standard, Exceeding the Standard) or reporting grades as 1, 2, 3, and 4
- ▶ use of median or mode to determine a grade
- ▶ grades entered into grade books as formative and summative under a particular standard

In schools that have moved to standards-based grade reporting, the trappings of traditional grading *systems* may still be in place. Some of these schools may still use class ranking and honor rolls and, most often, may still average grades. Yet, there are fewer barriers in moving from standards-based grading systems to competency-based grading systems because of the development of the underlying instruction and assessment components of standards-based teaching and learning.

COMPETENCY-BASED GRADING

The Bucket Theory of Competency-Based Grading

In a competency-based grading system, we want to track student performance over time with *rolling grades*, that is, grades not delineated by artificial time barriers such as the ends of quarters. We can think of this design as the bucket theory. For example, the competency for informational writing is essentially the same competency across grade levels, with increasing levels of complexity and, therefore, an expectation that the performance indicators over time would reflect this complexity. The competency for informational writing is one of the buckets in this new grading system. As the student produces evidence in written products, the teacher enters the grade for each item in the bucket for informational writing. Over time, the bucket becomes filled with evidence (grades) that reflect student proficiency in informational writing. A quick dipstick into the bucket would give anyone—teacher, parent, student, administrator—a relative sense of the learner's competency in informational writing. Essentially, this bucket is open and remains open throughout grades K–12. The view into the bucket will always be the latest, best interpretation of how the student writes. In looking at the bucket of information, the observer needs to discriminate the information carefully.

Averaging all the scores in the competency bucket would not be an accurate reflection of student learning, because early scores for writing can influence the overall grade. Nor would the average reflect the student's latest demonstrated performance level in writing. The best interpretation of the bucket of scores may be in the most recent scores entered or possibly the most frequent score present in the bucket. As described above, the bucket is open and stays open. For example, for the informational text competency, the scores on informational text writing may be gathered from September to June across one school year and reported to parents along the way. With competency-based grading, the parent can see the current year's performance in the informational text competency and will have access to previous competency grades. The student's grades across many years are readily available to the student's learning team at any time. Those scores are never archived or unavailable, because they are part of a historical record. Essentially, a report card can be generated easily on any day that one views the grades, which are housed in the system by competency. A district can adopt the same set of academic competencies from kindergarten to twelfth grade, and the bucket of grades for each competency just grows over time.

> The purpose of competency-based grading is to effectively communicate a learner's performance and competency in a valid, transparent, and coherent way. Competency-based grading communicates college and career readiness along the pathways of learning from elementary to middle school and finally to high school and graduation.

MOVING FROM TRADITIONAL TO COMPETENCY-BASED GRADING

There are challenges in changing traditional grading systems. As mentioned, this type of systemic change, when done too quickly or prematurely, can have negative consequences. One way to approach moving to competency-based grading is to do so in stages or phases of development. Most traditional grading systems never define the criteria for the letter grades A, B, C, D, and F. This is an ideal place to consider some early work in moving your grading system forward. You may also have number ranges associated with these grades in your system. You will have more work to do in moving to competency-based grading if you are using a hundred-point numerical scale than if you are using only a letter system. Consider using table 7.1 to make a few minor changes first. This first change maintains the same letter and number equivalent in the traditional system for grades A, B, and C. However, it introduces the concept that anything below a C communicates that the student is Not Yet Competent.

TABLE 7.1   First steps in moving from traditional to competency-based grading

FROM	TO
A (90–100)	A (90–100)
B (80–89)	B (80–89)
C (70–79)	C (70–79)
D (60–69)	NYC (Not Yet Competent)
F (below 69)	NYC (Not Yet Competent)

In taking the first step, teachers and administrators begin to address the problem of providing resources for students to reach the C grade. One of the early conversations should be how the school uses its grade-reporting system to determine as early as possible when a student may not be performing at the C level. How these students engage in reteaching and relearning to maintain the C level should be addressed with schoolwide resources rather than by each teacher charged with the responsibility of tracking these students and providing relearning and reassessment opportunities. With this first step in moving to competency-based grading, you communicate that anything less than a C does not represent acceptable performance criteria. The public understands this idea fairly easily. Would you want your physician, accountant, or car mechanic to work on you or your property, having passed a course with a 60?

The next phase of developing a competency-based grade-reporting system is to consider developing proficiency scales for grading. Table 5.2 describes in detail three proficiency scales with performance descriptors for each category: Competent with Distinction, Competent, and Not Yet Competent. Before you try to convert your traditional A, B, C, D, or F with a hundred-point numerical scale into such a detailed proficiency scale, for the next iteration of your grading system, consider simply adding competency equivalence. Table 7.2 shows that if your traditional system is that A means 90–100, it also means Advanced Competency.

Once you move to this language in your grading system, you are then ready to go deeper into defining the performance criteria that define each of the grading categories used in your system, as shown in table 7.3. At this point in the

TABLE 7.2   Making the transition to competency language in a grading scale

FROM	TO
A (90–100)	A (90–100) Exemplary Competency; Advanced Competency; or Competent with Distinction
B (80–89)	B (80–89) Beyond Competent
C (70–79)	C (70–79) Competent; or Proficient
D (60–69)	Not Yet Competent (NYC); or Insufficient Evidence of Proficiency (INS)
F (below 69)	Not Yet Competent (NYC); or Insufficient Evidence of Proficiency (INS)

TABLE 7.3   Adding a holistic proficiency scale to a grading system

TRADITIONAL LETTER GRADING	COMPETENCY-BASED GRADING	HOLISTIC PROFICIENCY SCALE
A	A (Exemplary Competency; Advanced Competency; or Competent with Distinction)	Various indicators demonstrate that student can analyze and synthesize course content materials within the discipline and can extend conceptual understanding to other disciplines. Various indicators demonstrate that the student clearly and effectively communicates his or her analytical and critical thinking, abstract reasoning, and problem solving with precision and accuracy within the content area.
B	B (Beyond Competent)	The student has a mixture of Competent and Advanced Competency indicators.
C	C (Competent; or Proficient)	Various indicators demonstrate the application and transfer of essential content and skills. There is sufficient evidence that the student effectively communicates his or her analytical and critical thinking, abstract reasoning, and problem solving with precision and accuracy within the content area.
D	Not Yet Competent (NYC); or Insufficient Evidence of Proficiency (INS)	There is insufficient evidence that the student can apply and transfer essential course content and skills. There is insufficient evidence that the student effectively communicates analytical, critical, abstract thinking, and problem solving with precision and accuracy within the content area.
F	Not Yet Competent (NYC); or Insufficient Evidence of Proficiency (INS)	

development of your competency-based grading system, there will need to be substantial time and effort in researching and developing the language most appropriate to define your holistic grading scale. It is very important to be mindful of the language in the proficiency scale so that parents understand what it means. Table 7.3 shows the further evolution to a competency-based grading scale by dropping the associated number scale. Your grading scale descriptors should be included on your report cards as a frame of reference for both parents and students.

As shown in table 7.2, one might argue that 70 is a low grade for competency. But if you are moving from a traditional grading system, you should begin with such a hybrid grading system, which includes letter grades and numbers and a proficiency scale, as well as the holistic proficiency scale, which explains the competency-based system. Eventually, you will drop the numerical scale. We have found that when you start tuning your task rubrics to a proficiency scale, you will be increasing the demands for rigor in student performance. That is an adjustment for teachers, students, and parents.

When transforming the grading system in the Rochester School District, my colleagues and I found it difficult to define a grade of B. We could describe A and C easily, but B was a bit elusive. Table 7.3 shows how to arrive at a grade of B in a competency scale by citing the holistic proficiency scale for grades A and C. Having a clear holistic proficiency scale can help you make these determinations once you have set aside your numerical system.

When teachers bring their district's holistic proficiency scale descriptors into their grading rubrics, it makes sense. As they use a rubric to look at a student's work, they may score some pieces of work Competent and other pieces Advanced Competency. When this happens, a grade of B, or Beyond Competent, is entered.

Schools and districts must report and subsequently transcribe student learning reliably in communicating the full breadth of student proficiency and growth in personal success skills, especially when considering that report cards and transcripts are used by other institutions and workplaces. We should also be careful to communicate student learning clearly, because some students move from school to school, across state borders, and even internationally. For this reason, competency-based grading must be coherent in its design, especially in the use of proficiency scales for grades K–12.

In changing a grading system from traditional to competency based, be mindful of the students experiencing those shifts. How can we best design coherent grading systems so that the change would cause the fewest problems for the students? One district chose a time-based strategic three-year plan to move to competency-based grading. As a result, the students were graded three different ways across those three years. To avoid problems like this, educators should not try to propose grading system changes without walking the walk of students moving through those changes.

The Sanborn Regional School District intentionally planned its move to competency-based grading by continually adding *more* information to its report cards. It began with the typical hundred-point numerical scale and letter-grade system. It then started adding competency-based grades to the report card. Over time, the district culled the letter and number grading information so that, after several years, only letter grading remained.

Public schools face a heavier burden in planning the shift to competency-based grading. Often, charter and independent schools can open their doors with competency-based or alternative grading systems already in place. In the public arena, however, I have found that in larger K–12 systems, more time is needed to create the firm foundation in competency design, performance assessment, and new learning pathways before grading changes can be introduced. In addition, the replacement or addition of large-scale management software to support and adequately communicate learning through CBE criteria requires a multiyear study with the attendant budgetary considerations. Moving to competency-based grading is a cultural change and, as such, cannot be introduced as if it were a new program or initiative. It is inexorably connected to instruction and learning, and until those new competency-based teaching and learning opportunities are ingrained into the culture of a school, competency-based grading just doesn't make sense.

On the other hand, this type of grading makes more sense for learners if it is introduced by grade span early on and if the grading changes move with the students through the system. The language of the full breadth of tools—personal learning plans, learning management system information, academic proficiency information, personal success skills development—grows with the students as they grow through the system. It is open for the entire time.

At the beginning of CBE reform at Lebanon High School, Nan Parsons, the principal of the school, worked for a year with eighth-grade parents and teachers to explain that when the children entered the high school, their courses would be competency based. The adults were introduced to the high school's new grading philosophy, which was developed after teachers conducted research on the best practices in grading. Once the course competencies were designed and validated, the teachers had formulated how they would grade student work against the competencies using the grading scales defined in the grading philosophy statement. There was no attempt to move the whole high school to the new competency-based system. As that cohort of students moved through the high school, teachers in the next grade level up took on the new grading system. While the students saw no change in their own learning and assessment from grades 9 to 12, they essentially changed the school's system as they moved through school. This approach also added in the development work in course competencies and performance assessment over several years.

A great analogy for designing such an open system is the current digital medical records system used by most medical practices. In such a system, a patient has an identifying number that is used to connect all medical information over time. The record, once open, literally stays open and grows with the patient. If the patient is hospitalized, the doctors treating the patient and all the clinical tests move into the patient's medical records. Every medical test, prescription, and practitioner becomes part of the patient's total clinical picture over many years. As with the medical industry, we need to have open systems of student information that is easily accessible by educators, parents, and students to make the best decisions on learning throughout the K–12 experience.

A pressure point in this work is to demand this type of openness from the management software that typically runs our schools today. For far too long, we have based our grading practices on what the software can do instead of design in a grading program to accurately and comprehensively report multiple measures of learning for students across the entire journey from kindergarten to twelfth grade. Let's look at what a good competency-based grading system should do.

What Is an A?

In most traditional grading systems, the hundred-point numerical scale and letter grades are used in grading student work. However, rarely does a school or district define what a student must do, or what level of student performance is expected, for any of the grades. This lack of clarity leads to a great deal of unreliability in grading.

Competency-based grading systems must be built in such a way that every grade communicates performance on an agreed-on definition of competency. Schools and districts must agree on what constitutes the proficiency scale in their grading system. Thomas Guskey firmly contends and has proven that the hundred-point scale should not be used in grading systems, because it is unfair and unreliable.[1] This numerical scale may give the illusion of precision, but grading on this scale is subjective and unreliable. Guskey's research clearly indicates that the large number of grade categories on the hundred-point scale requires fine discrimination to determine the difference from one grade point to the next.

Often in traditional grading systems, we can distinguish between an A, a B, or a C, but rarely do we discriminate the criteria between a 90, 91, or 92 or any other points in the hundred-point scale. Those fine number discriminations are often left to the teacher's own subjectivity and judgment, which may be very different from those of another teacher looking at the same piece of work. This type of grading error from paper to paper, and from student to student, contributes to the diminished reliability of any grade determined using a hundred-point scale. Guskey further adds that the hundred-point scale gives the illusion of precision when, in fact, it is exactly the opposite. With a reduced scoring range typically found in standards-based and competency-based grading, there is greater agreement in comparative scoring. Given performance descriptors for the four grading categories, a student's work can be examined and graded with greater precision and reliability because the discrimination between the performance criteria is made more easily and with greater reliability by multiple scorers. These benefits become evident when groups of teachers conduct double scoring of writing samples using a four-point rubric.

Decreasing the points in a grading scale would increase precision and reliability and more accurately reflect student performance. For this reason, many standards-based and competency-based grading systems usually use only four or five grading categories. But how do you change a system that has been firmly entrenched in the hundred-point numerical scale?

We've solved this problem in several systems by adding a frame of reference for competency grades over time, moving away from the hundred-point scale entirely. For example, table 7.4 shows the grading scale used by the Epping School District in New Hampshire.[2]

The work in the Epping School District is like the efforts in several other schools that have embraced this work and are moving forward in their thinking. The district established several good foundational considerations when it began developing a competency-based grading system over time. Because the hundred-point scale has been firmly entrenched both in teacher practice and in parent understanding (and demand) of grading, the district includes this scale

TABLE 7.4 Epping, New Hampshire, school district grading scale and definitions

LEVEL OF COMPETENCY	OVERALL COURSE GRADE	COMPETENCY CONTENT GRADE	COMPETENCY SKILL GRADE	EQUIVALENT NUMBER GRADE	TRADITIONAL LETTER GRADE	PERFORMANCE DESCRIPTORS FOR COURSE AND DISTRICT COMPETENCIES
Advanced	A+ to A-	A+ to A-	4	90–100	A+ to A-	The student consistently exceeds the performance standards for the grade level. Understands and applies key concepts and skills with consistency and independence.
Beyond competent	B+ to B-	B+ to B-	3	80–89	B+ to B-	The student consistently meets the performance standards for the grade level. Understands and applies key concepts and skills with consistency and effectiveness.
Competent	C+ to C-	C+ to C-	2	70–79	C+ to C-	The student has a general understanding of the performance standards for the grade level. Understands key concepts and skills and is working on applying concepts and skills.
Not Yet competent	N	N	1	Below 70	D to F	Student does not yet understand key concepts and skills and is working toward this goal.
Not assessed	NA	NA	NA			The standard has not yet been assessed.
Incomplete	I	I	I			Incomplete grade due to extenuating circumstances.

(centered yet separated from the newer parts of the system) on its report cards, thereby retaining a frame of reference for parents (see table 7.4). Epping teachers have worked very hard to develop formative and summative assessments using the performance descriptors for their course and district competencies. They have moved this work into their framework for the New Hampshire PACE (see chapter 10). In fact, each unit of work developed as part of the high school curriculum is mapped to the district competencies for ease in grading.

Table 7.4 shows the relationship between the competency-based indicators, the relative scale, and the traditional scale—a perfect example of melding the old and the new. If I were to predict how Epping will develop its future grading system, I would expect the district to reduce the plus-and-minus features of its letter and number grades and then to eventually eliminate its number system. Slowly, over time, a new culture of competency-based grading will endure. Note that the district philosophically adhered to the concept that a D in the traditional system has no merit. Competency is all about performance that meets criteria of acceptable proficiency.

What does this story tell us? It speaks to the realistic growth curve in moving grading systems forward. It says that we must first be honest about the system that is currently in place and that grounds us as educators in a history of communicating student learning. We should fight the compulsion to be reductionist in CBE, especially in grading. The more information, curated for precision and reliability around matters that count, that parents have, the more they can understand how their children are growing in competency. Superimposing a competency grading system on top of the existing traditional system and then helping parents understand how the additional information further informs them about their child in meaningful ways builds parental support for the change. The idea that competency-based grading must be recorded as a 1, 2, 3, 4 system or that it doesn't report grades is a misconception. Brian Stack, principal of Sanborn Regional High School, addresses some misconceptions about competency-based grading in "Voices from the Field: Separating Fact from Myth in the Competency-Based High School Transcript."

Many high school parents fear that the movement to a different grading system will disadvantage their children when they apply to college. It is our responsibility to inform parents that a CBE transcript communicates more than do traditional transcripts. Many parents of students in traditional high schools somehow feel that the rest of the world operates the way their own high school does—they are unaware of the great variety of application materials that colleges receive from students in all sorts of educational environments. In any given admissions class, home-schoolers and students from international schools, charter schools, independent schools, and online schools are all vying for admission, and each applicant presents a very different profile. School leaders should be prepared for this question when speaking with parents and community members.

Parents concerned about the issue of college applications maybe be reassured to realize that the structure and operation of many colleges and universities is also changing. The Competency-Based Education Network (www.cbenetwork. org) is at the forefront of helping colleges and universities move toward CBE. Southern New Hampshire University has been a pioneer and a national model in offering competency-based degree programs in its College for America, a partnership between the university and various US businesses to offer students more workplace-applicable competencies in their college degrees.

Currently, sixty-seven colleges and universities in New England have signed on to a memorandum of understanding with the New England Secondary School Consortium in support of CBE and nontraditional grade and transcript reporting.[3] The New England Board of Higher Education has created a white paper in collaboration with the consortium, reporting that students who graduate from or competency-based high schools are at no disadvantage in the college admission process.[4] Simply stated, the landscape of the college admissions experience is changing, and parents need to be informed about this.

Even among students from traditional high schools, colleges must sift through a variety of grading systems to determine which applicants will be the best fit for their institutions. Many parents feel that their children must be exceptional on all fronts to compete for admission. Yet on the other side of the process, colleges are seeking the best students to be successful in *their* settings. This is a huge disconnect and one that high school guidance counselors need to address with parents, who may be fixated on the statistics of GPAs, class standings, and SAT or ACT results. Counselors should stress to parents that they need to know how their students rate on the nonacademic college- and career-readiness skills. Their children's future success may be firmly grounded in those skills in addition to their GPAs in academic areas. In fact, the child's college- and career-readiness profile may help a family decide whether a college experience away from home is a better choice than a gap-year experience. For some children, the latter may be a better choice if they need to grow developmentally to function independently in the rigorous performance expectations of higher education.

Brian Stack has been a strong national voice on the many ways in which the shift to competency-based grading has improved the culture for teaching and learning in his school. In "Voices from the Field: Separating Fact from Myth in the Competency-Based High School Transcript," he uncovers several myths and misconceptions that are important to dispel if we educators are to engage staff and parents in conversations about a better grading system.

VOICES FROM THE FIELD
SEPARATING FACT FROM MYTH IN THE COMPETENCY-BASED HIGH SCHOOL TRANSCRIPT

By Brian Stack, principal of Sanborn Regional High School, Kingston, New Hampshire

After many years of experience as a high school principal in a competency-based high school, I have found that it is the transcript that generates the most inquiry from outsiders seeking to understand our system, and for good reason. In both traditional and competency-based models, the high school transcript represents a student's ultimate cumulative record of learning, a record that must be communicated clearly and concisely to both admissions officers at postsecondary institutions and potential employers. Over the years, I have encountered several misconceptions and myths about what a transcript for a competency-based program should look like. It's time to dispel these myths and set the record straight.

MYTH: Reporting measures such as grade point average (GPA) and class rank cannot be computed in a competency-based school.

False. These two measures *can* be included on a competency-based transcript. Outsiders and newcomers often worry that because most competency-based schools report assignment grades using a four- or five-point letter rubric scale, you cannot compute a GPA. This is simply not true. In my school, a student can only earn one of five letter grades on individual assignments, according to their performance level as indicated on a rubric, but in the background, those letters correlate to the numerical values of 0, 1, 2, 3, or 4. As the student completes multiple assignments, we can compute an overall course grade and thus a GPA that is a numerical value between 0 and 4. From the GPA, it is then easy to compute a class rank statistic. This, however, leads to another popular myth.

> **MYTH:** Competency-based schools do not want to report class rank, because it doesn't fit with their philosophy.

This statement is true, but most competency-based high schools continue to report class rank because it is a statistic that many admissions offices still seek from applicants. Philosophically, class rank doesn't fit with the competency education model, because it is computed by comparing an individual's performance against the performance of his or her peers. Class rank gives no indication of the level or degree of learning that has taken place. In competency-based systems, student learning is measured against a standard of performance set forth in a well-defined rubric. Although the tide is starting to turn, this philosophy is not yet widespread in higher education, and thus class rank is still a standard reporting measure that competency-based high schools calculate and report.

> **MYTH:** In a competency-based school, the transcript is too long and thus too confusing for college admissions officers and potential employers to follow, because it contains much more detail than one from a traditional school has.

False. Most competency-based high school transcripts still contain the same basic reporting measures, which include course names, final course grades, credit earned, GPA, and class rank. Over the years, I have shared our transcripts with hundreds of admissions officers representing postsecondary institutions from coast to coast. I have yet to encounter one who was confused by our transcript or our competency-based reporting model. For many outsiders new to the competency education approach, this knowledge brings about a welcome sigh of relief. Many parents and students fear that if their high school were to move to such a model, the transcript would change so drastically that it would be difficult to interpret and thus hurt a student's chances of being accepted to a postsecondary institution or being offered a job. I have not seen this problem at all. In my school, for the ten years before the implementation of competency education, an average of 72 percent of our graduates attended two- or four-year colleges after high school. In the six years since the implementation, the statistic has risen to nearly 78 percent. The implementation hasn't hurt the students' chances of staying in college, either. Since we started collecting data on our graduates in 2013, we know that, on average, 87 percent of them return for a second year of college, a statistic far above the national average.

In my experience, I have come to understand that reporting on student learning in a competency-based model has several layers. At the assignment level, rubrics help students understand how their learning meets or exceeds the performance criteria set for the competency or skill or skills being assessed. At the course level, a report card communicates to students their performance on each of the competencies associated with the course of study. The transcript simply gives a high-level overview of performance in each course of study over a student's entire high school career. The role of the transcript has not changed, and its format doesn't have to, either.

From Brian Stack, "Separating the Facts from the Myths in the Competency-Based High School Transcript," *CompetencyWorks* (blog), September 12, 2016, www.competencyworks.org /understanding-competency-education/separating-the-facts-from-the-myths-in-the-competency -based-high-school-transcript. Reprinted with permission.

With seven elementary schools, one large middle school, and one large high school, the Rochester School District is an exemplar of an urban school district. It began its journey in CBE by first working for several years to develop high-quality course competencies at the high school level in response to the state mandate to have those in place by the 2008 academic year. Shortly thereafter, the district began to develop its competency-based grading system. Spaulding High School began this work by developing its grading philosophy statement, a single K–12 report card that combines reports on progress toward competencies and personal success skills. This was a prolonged process of working with individual departments and faculty on the shifts in instruction and ideology needed to support competency-based learning, assessment, and grading. The high school used the grading philosophy statement in its grading practices for approximately two years before K–8 began using it. During those two years, through summer sessions called competency camps, teachers began to align their competency statements and performance indicators to the Common Core State Standard and their grading rubrics. A great deal of professional development time was spent in reworking the assessments found in the elementary reading and mathematics programs. Many of the program assessments fell short of the needed DOK level required to demonstrate proficiency.

As shown in the chapter appendix, Rochester approached its transformation to CBE comprehensively. This policy has guided teacher practice over several years, grounding teachers new to the district in a uniform orientation in grading. The grading system was incorporated into the district's student information system at great cost and effort, but it was a good investment. Visit the district's website (www.rochesterschools.com) to explore Rochester's grade-level competencies and performance indicators to see how the district structured its grading into its individual competency rubrics. In carrying its holistic grading rubric through to the design of its individual competencies with performance indicators, the district took a powerful step in developing grading coherence across grade levels and within courses.

This transition has been a work in progress and will continue to be in the years to come. One aspect of Rochester's developmental work in 2016 was to add more rigor to the performance assessments that are graded as Competent.

Blueprint for Designing Your Competency-Based Grading System

In moving toward CBE, many of your designs must be integrative. If you are designing competencies, for example, you think about how they will be supported and used in your assessment and grading systems. In thinking about how your students grow through your system, you think about proficiency scales that teachers use to grade papers from kindergarten to twelfth grade. If you are moving from standards-based to competency-based grading, you think of the professional development that teachers will need to change how they enter grades in grade books.

The following lists are a blueprint for you to consider as you begin to move your district toward competency-based grading. For you, the steps may not be in the same order, or you may wish to design toward a particular grading system to communicate student learning. The blueprint aims to reinforce the importance of integrating competency design, performance assessment, learning growth along different pathways over time, and communicating college- and career-readiness development over time.

Prerequisites for Competency-Based Grading
- Design and validate competencies for use in your system.
- Plan long-term professional learning in assessment literacy to design high-quality performance tasks and assessment rubrics incorporating DOK.

Designing Your Proficiency Scales and Grading Criteria
- Create your holistic proficiency scales.
- Provide professional learning opportunities to examine student work using teacher-created rubrics based on the holistic proficiency scale.

Designing Your Report Card
- Design a K–12 report card.
- Prominently display the purpose for the report card.
- Include your grading scales and criteria for the grades on the report card.
- Include reporting of personal success skills separately from academic grade reporting.

Technology Considerations
- Engage both teachers and technology staff in discussion on choice of software that supports the competency-based grading system.
- Begin technology considerations early in the process for budget planning purposes.

Designing and implementing a competency-based grading system is difficult work. It is politically charged and affects teachers' grading practices. But when done well, it will create the evidence-based information system needed to communicate college and career readiness.

ADDITIONAL RESOURCES

Dueck, Myron. *Grading Smarter, Not Harder: Assessment Strategies That Motivate Kids and Help Them Learn.* Alexandria, VA: Association for Supervision & Curriculum Development, 2014.

Erickson, Jeffrey. "Grading Practices: The Third Rail." *Principal Leadership* (2010): 22–26.

Guskey, Thomas R. "Helping Standards Make the Grade." *Educational Leadership* 59, no. 1 (2001): 20–27.

———. "Making High School Grades Meaningful." *Phi Delta Kappan* (2006): 670–75.

———. "Making the Grade: What Benefits Student." *Educational Leadership* 52, no. 2 (1994): 14–20.

———. *Practical Solutions for Serious Problems in Standards-Based Grading.* Thousand Oaks, CA: Corwin Press, 2008.

———. "The Case Against Percentage Grades." *Educational Leadership* 71, no. 1 (2013): 68–72.

Guskey, Thomas R., and Jane M. Bailey. *Developing Grading and Reporting Systems for Student Learning: Experts in Assessment.* Thousand Oaks, CA: Corwin Press, 2001.

———. *Developing Standards-Based Report Cards.* Thousand Oaks, CA: Corwin Press, 2009.

Guskey, Thomas R., and L. Jung. "Grading and Reporting Student Learning." 2007. http://docushare.everett.k12.wa.us/docushare/dsweb/Get/Document-15427/Guskey%20Grading4%20lrng%20Binder.pdf&oi=ggp.

Heflebower, Tammy, Jan K. Hoegh, and Phil Warrick. *A School Leader's Guide to Standards-Based Grading.* Bloomington, IN: Marzano Research Laboratory, 2014.

Marzano, Robert J. *Transforming Classroom Grading.* Alexandria, VA: Association for Supervision & Curriculum Development, 2000.

———. *Classroom Assessment & Grading That Work.* Alexandria, VA: Association for Supervision & Curriculum Development, 2006.

O'Connor, Kenneth. "The Principal's Role in Report Card Grading." *NASSP Bulletin* 85, no. 621 (2001): 37.

———. *How to Grade for Learning, K–12.* Thousand Oaks, CA: Corwin Press, 2009.

O'Connor, Kenneth, and R. J. Stiggins. *How to Grade for Learning: Linking Grades to Standards*. Thousand Oaks, CA: Corwin Press, 2002.

Reeves, Douglas. *Elements of Grading: A Guide to Effective Practice*. Bloomington, IN: Solution Tree, 2010.

Scriffiny, Patricia. "Seven Reasons for Standards-Based Grading." *Educational Leadership* 66, no. 2 (2008): 70–74.

Wormeli, Rick. *Fair Isn't Always Equal*. Portland, ME: Stenhouse Publishers, 2006.

Appendix (Chapter 7)

Rochester School District Competency-Based Assessment and Grading Philosophy Statement

PURPOSE

In the Rochester School District, assessment and grading have many purposes: providing feedback to students, parents, and teachers, documenting student progress, and guiding instructional decisions. In a competency-based system, instruction and assessment are driven by course-defined competency statements and performance indicators.

COMPETENCY STATEMENT & PERFORMANCE INDICATORS DEFINED

Competency is a mastery of knowledge and content in a setting that requires a student to apply learning within or across content domains. A competency statement speaks to the overarching enduring understandings that a student gains as a result of active learning. From the student perspective, the competency statement really answers the question: "Why are you asking me to learn this?" Teachers in the Rochester School District have developed competencies in each of the content areas. Grade-level and course competencies are consistent across the district. These competencies are driven by national, state, and local standards.

Each competency has multiple performance indicators that are assessed to determine student mastery. Performance indicators are the specific measurable stages of student achievement. They describe what the students should know and be able to do. Performance indicators are a demonstration of a student's learned concepts, content, and skills. A student's level of competence is determined by the assessment results from the performance indicators.

ASSESSMENT RUBRICS & GRADING SCALES

Teachers will report student progress in core courses using the grade-specific mastery rubric outlined below and will also report on *Habits of Engaged Learners* (see end of document). A student's grades will represent his/her level of mastery toward reaching the defined competencies. Extra credit (i.e., bringing in an item for the food drive, bonus points on a test, or attending a school event) will not be used in determining a student's academic grade.

K–8

Student assessments will be scored Exceeds Competent (E), Competent (C), Not Yet Competent (NYC) or Insufficient Work Submitted (IWS) and will also report on *Habits of Engaged Learners* (see end of document).

E Exceeds Competent	C Competent	NYC Not Yet Competent	IWS Insufficient Work Submitted
In addition to Competent: Extends knowledge and skills beyond essential content knowledge and skills.	Essential content knowledge and skills are demonstrated consistently and student applies content and skills using strategic thinking.	Essential content knowledge and skills are demonstrated inconsistently, incompletely, or inaccurately.	Insufficient evidence is submitted to measure competence.

4–12

Student assessments will be scored Advanced (A), Beyond Competent (B), Competent (C), Not Yet Competent (NYC) or Insufficient Work Submitted (IWS) and will also report on *Habits of Engaged Learners* (see end of document).

A Advanced Competent	B Beyond Competent	C Competent	NYC Not Yet Competent	IWS Insufficient Work Submitted
In addition to Beyond Competent: Extends understanding of essential content and skills using other content areas and real-world applications.	In addition to Competent: Essential content and skills are extended with increased complexity and depth of understanding.	Essential content knowledge and skills are demonstrated consistently. Applies content and skills using strategic thinking.	Essential content knowledge and skills are demonstrated inconsistently, incompletely or inaccurately.	Insufficient evidence is submitted to measure competence.

ASSESSMENT RUBRICS & GRADING SCALES

UNIFIED ARTS ASSESSMENT RUBRICS & GRADING SCALES

K–8

Elementary Level: Music, Art and Physical Education and *Middle School Level*: Quarter-long exploratory classes (General Music, Art, Physical Education, Computer Technology, Family & Consumer Science, Exploratory Modern & Classical Languages, Health, and Vocational Education) will be scored Exceeds Competent (E), Competent (C), Not Yet Competent (NYC) or Insufficient Work Submitted (IWS) and will also report on *Habits of Engaged Learners* (see end of document).

E Exceeds Competent	C Competent	NYC Not Yet Competent	IWS Insufficient Work Submitted
In addition to Competent: Extends knowledge and skills beyond essential content knowledge and skills.	Essential content knowledge and skills are demonstrated consistently and student applies content and skills using strategic thinking.	Essential content knowledge and skills are demonstrated inconsistently, incompletely or inaccurately.	Insufficient evidence is submitted to measure competence.

6–8

Student assessments for full year courses (Chorus, Band, French I and Spanish I) will be scored Advanced (A), Beyond Competent (B), Competent (C), Not Yet Competent (NYC) or Insufficient Work Submitted (IWS) and will also report on *Habits of Engaged Learners* (see end of document).

A Advanced Competent	B Beyond Competent	C Competent	NYC Not Yet Competent	IWS Insufficient Work Submitted
In addition to Beyond Competent: Extends understanding of essential content and skills using other content areas and real-world applications.	In addition to Competent: Essential content and skills are extended with increased complexity and depth of understanding.	Essential content knowledge and skills are demonstrated consistently. Applies content and skills using strategic thinking.	Essential content knowledge and skills are demonstrated inconsistently, incompletely or inaccurately.	Insufficient evidence is submitted to measure competence.

REPORTING ON STUDENT ACHIEVEMENT

Student achievement will be reported through progress reports and report cards. In addition, parents can use the Infinite Campus Parent Portal to monitor their child's progress. Each progress report or portal check-in is a "snapshot" of where a student is on his/her learning journey.

K–3 The competency report card will communicate a student's achievement by competency for each area of study at regular intervals and a final competency grade at the end of the year.

4–8 The competency report card will communicate a student's achievement by competency for each area of study at regular intervals and a final competency grade at the end of the year. The report card will also communicate an overall "snapshot" for each core area of study and report a final grade at the end of the year. Unified Arts courses will communicate a student's achievement by competency.

9–12 The competency report card will regularly communicate a student's achievement by competency, for each area of study. The report card will also communicate a student's final course grade. In a competency-based course, a student gains credit only with the demonstration of mastery.

Courses at the high school level are weighted. This weighting is used to calculate the grade point average (GPA). GPA is the total number of grade points accumulated using a weighted scale, divided by the total number of credits attempted. This weighted scale is designed to acknowledge students who challenge themselves by taking more rigorous classes. A student's class rank is determined by their cumulative GPA.

TYPES OF ASSESSMENT

Throughout the year, the student will have multiple and varied opportunities to demonstrate progress toward mastery of course competencies. This is accomplished through formative and summative assessments that are aligned with performance indicators.

FORMATIVE ASSESSMENT *FOR LEARNING*

In order for a teacher to measure student progress toward mastery of performance indicators, formative assessments are used to gauge student understanding and to provide feedback for further learning. Formative assessments are informative for the teacher; the teacher uses the student learning data gained from formative assessments to shape his/her instruction for the students. These assessments help students move forward in their learning toward a specific goal and measure individual progress. Examples include, but are not limited to, teacher observation, verbal and written checks, activities that reinforce skills, small daily quizzes, worksheets and practice exercises. This type of assessment is used for planning appropriate instruction for students as they learn. *Formative assessment is weighted no more than 10% of a student's grade (K–8) and no more than 25% with 10% required from homework of a student's grade (9–12).*

SUMMATIVE ASSESSMENT *OF LEARNING*

In order to measure a student's mastery of the competencies, summative assessments are used. Summative assessments provide cumulative data that indicate the level of student learning for reporting purposes. They allow teachers to make judgments about student achievement at the end of a sequence of instruction. Summative assessment tools may include tests, quizzes, projects, performances and/or products. These assessments are rigorous and include a variety of opportunities to demonstrate depth of knowledge. *Summative assessment is weighted no less than 90% of a student's grade (K–8) and no less than 75% of a student's grade (9–12).*

RELEARNING AND REASSESSMENT OPPORTUNITIES

The Rochester School District recognizes that students learn at different rates; therefore, they will be provided with summative relearning opportunities that begin in the classroom with differentiated instruction and further assessment.

K–5

The relearning and reassessment processes may take several forms, as determined by the classroom teacher; additional resources may include intervention teachers or an individualized plan based on the student's needs. For example, the student, with the teacher's assistance and guidance, may demonstrate competence in the area of need or the student may require more intensive instruction. *The reassessment grade will replace the previous grade.*

FINAL GRADES K–3

Students receiving a majority of Not Yet Competent (NYC) and/or Insufficient Work Submitted (IWS) final grades in reading and/or mathematics competencies will be required to participate in tiered intervention programs, before/after school programming and/or a school-sponsored summer program before being promoted to the next grade.

If, after participating in these programs, the student still has not demonstrated competency, the school will develop a plan to address these areas of academic need either in the next grade or through retention. The principal has the final say in grade level placement.

FINAL GRADES 4–5

In order to be promoted to the next grade, students need to demonstrate competency in all core academic areas (reading, English/language arts, mathematics, science and social studies). A student who has not demonstrated competency in the academic core as reflected in his/her final overall grades will be required to attend a competency completion program to be considered for promotion. This may include participation in the school's summer program.

If a student does not demonstrate competency by the end of the summer program, the school will develop a plan which will outline how the student will reach competency. This plan may require retention. The principal has the final say in grade level placement.

Relearning opportunities will be facilitated by the classroom teacher; additional resources may include intervention teachers, online learning opportunities, or an individualized plan based on the student's needs. Reassessment opportunities do not necessarily duplicate the design of the original assessment. Reassessments are given once relearning has occurred and communication with parent/guardian has taken place. *The reassessment grade will replace the previous grade.*

The relearning process may take several forms, as determined by the teacher. The teacher will design a relearning plan with the student, which will be communicated to the parent/guardian. For example, a completion calendar may be created outlining what relearning will be done within an agreed-upon time frame.

FINAL GRADES 6–8

In order to be promoted to the next grade, students need to demonstrate competency in all core academic areas (reading, English/language arts, mathematics, science and social studies). A student who has not demonstrated competency in the academic core as reflected in his/her final overall grades will be required to attend a competency completion program to be considered for promotion. This may include participation in the school's summer program.

If a student does not demonstrate competency by the end of the summer program, the school will develop a plan which will outline how the student will reach competency. This plan may require retention. The principal has the final say in grade level placement.

Relearning opportunities will be co-planned by the classroom teacher and student; additional resources may include intervention teachers, online learning opportunities, or an individualized plan facilitated through Alternative Pathways, based on the student's needs. Relearning and reassessment opportunities do not necessarily duplicate the design of the original learning or assessment. Reassessments are given once relearning has occurred and communication with parent/guardian has taken place. *The reassessment grade will replace the previous grade.*

The teacher will design a relearning plan with the student that will be communicated to the parent/guardian.

FINAL COURSE GRADES 9–12

Relearning opportunities are required for students who receive a class/course grade of Not Yet Competent (NYC). A plan with an identified timeline for completion will be developed for all students earning an NYC. If the established timeline is not adhered to and there are no extenuating circumstances, the NYC will be changed to an F. The length of the timeline will be as short as possible and should not exceed one semester and one summer from the time the NYC is received. If a student with an NYC retakes the course, the NYC will be changed to an F for the previous course.

Upon graduation from the Rochester School District, any remaining NYC's will be converted to an F. Students who do not submit sufficient evidence to measure competence will receive a class/course grade of Insufficient Work Submitted (IWS). Students earning an IWS will be required to repeat the course and the final grade will be converted to an F.

CRITERIA FOR REASSESSMENT

Note: The reassessment grade will replace the previous grade.

	ORIGINAL GRADE	ELIGIBLE FOR REASSESSMENT	NUMBER OF POSSIBLE REASSESSMENTS	POSSIBLE GRADES
K–5	Not Yet Competent (NYC)	Yes	As many opportunities as needed for a student to reach competent. Once the student reaches competent, he/she may have one more opportunity to exceed competent.	E, C or NYC (K–3) A, B, C or NYC (4–5)
	B (4–5) or C (K-5)	Yes	One additional opportunity to exceed competent.	E, C or NYC (K–3) A, B, C or NYC (4–5)
	ORIGINAL GRADE	ELIGIBLE FOR REASSESSMENT	NUMBER OF POSSIBLE REASSESSMENTS	POSSIBLE GRADES
6–8	Not Yet Competent (NYC)	Yes	As many opportunities as needed for a student to reach competent. Once the student reaches competent, he/she may have one more opportunity to exceed competent.	A, B, E (Unified Arts), C or NYC
	C	Yes	One additional opportunity to exceed competent.	A, B, E (Unified Arts), C or NYC
	B	Yes	One additional opportunity to exceed beyond competent.	A, B or NYC
	ORIGINAL GRADE	ELIGIBLE FOR REASSESSMENT	NUMBER OF POSSIBLE REASSESSMENTS	POSSIBLE GRADES
9–12	Not Yet Competent (NYC)	Yes	As many opportunities as needed for a student to reach competent. The reassessment will only be designed at the competent level.	C or NYC
	C	Yes	One additional opportunity to exceed competent. The reassessment will only be designed at the beyond competent level.	B, C or NYC
	B	Yes	One additional opportunity to exceed the beyond competent level. The reassessment will be designed at the advanced competent level.	A, B, C or NYC

Note: If a student's performance is lower on the reassessment than the original assessment, the teacher will need to analyze the results to determine why the student's learning regressed.

Chapter 8

Leadership

STRONG LEADERSHIP HAS ALWAYS been at the heart of productive school reform. Our new school leaders must be able to challenge the historical structure of existing roles within their schools. The typical job description of leaders in the traditional school model has to be reexamined in light of the need to meet this very different learning environment. Moving from the adult-centric work environment to a learner-centric one shifts adult roles significantly. It may be the most significant change in what school looks like within its walls and to the public. It will take a new kind of leader to think this through and lead this transformation.

One of the greatest challenges for educational leaders pursuing CBE is to garner the support for these efforts from community members. Principals often build support for school initiatives from within the community of students and their families. However, school transformation requires going to the broader community of businesspeople, retirees, and the growing population of adult single homes. Parents of homeschoolers and children attending charter schools may also financially support a public school that doesn't look, feel, or act like the school they received their education from years earlier. With the need to gain support from such a diverse community, school leaders need different approaches and skill sets from what they may currently have in their wheelhouses.

In the past ten years, I have worked with many district leadership teams from rural, suburban, and urban settings both small and large. Through all this work,

I come away convinced that the success of school transformation rests with capable, forward- thinking leaders.

The shifts to CBE to promote personalized learning must be supported by educational leaders who build the vision for the future and who design a framework for sustainability. If we as leaders move to CBE just because we think it is a promising trend, the effort will be reduced to another new initiative that will fall by the wayside with changes in leadership.

In 2016, I was contacted by a researcher for a consortium of superintendents from a state that was taking some initial steps in considering CBE. The researcher's goal was to present a report outlining how CBE is structured and concrete data to support its effectiveness. He was quite clear that unless he could produce a blueprint for reform and effectiveness data, the superintendents would not consider moving in that direction.

In a very long conversation, I pointed to evidence from Chugach, Sanborn, Lindsay Unified, and several other districts nationally moving toward CBE. My challenge in the conversation was to explain that moving to CBE isn't a one-size-fits-all process. It must be a responsive, customized school transformation. When done well, CBE will look different in different schools and districts. There are many portals of entry into this work, and they are based on the school's teaching and learning culture as well as the community setting for each school. CBE can sometimes look different even from school to school within one district. For this reason, it is difficult to use the same data points in determining effectiveness across different schools. Promising short-term results from this work will often then bring on expansion and further development. For example, in February 2013, Competency-Works reported that in Muscatine Iowa, no student earned grades of D or F in CBE classrooms, compared with 38 percent of all students in 2011–2012. Competency-Works also reported that after three years of the use of a performance-based system in Lindsay Unified School District in California, from 2009 to 2012, scores on the California Academic Performance Index increased by 91 percent.[1] This customization of school reform, rather than the imposition of a template of one-size-fits-all programming, is a hard concept to grapple with when we are thinking about school reform. Perhaps the researcher's group of superintendents might have been looking for multiple trajectories of new programs and approaches that each had data to signify that CBE works. It just doesn't work that way in practice. If we really want to do CBE well, there will emerge many pathways to student success, defined by our ability to dynamically meet student needs over time.

The reasons for moving to CBE should be local. Our learners, their social settings, the characteristics of the community, and our resources play into decisions about how to best engage and improve the current teaching and learning environments. In an urban high school that wants to reduce its dropout rate, personalization will look very different than it does in a traditional, high performing high school in a suburban setting. If the urban high school moves to personalized learning using personal learning plans and personal success skills, and it sees literacy and numeracy skills and dropout rates improve, that is the data point the school will use to discern its success. The suburban high school may use different criteria as its data point for interpreting success. This example describes both the need to design teaching and learning systems that are different from previous generations' systems and the frustration in finding the exact formula for successful transformation to CBE. The transformation will look different from community to community, but sharing our approaches in the journey toward personalized, competency-based learning can inform all our thinking about the work. One constant is this: educational leadership plays a central role in the successful transformation to CBE.

THE LENS OF LEADERSHIP IN COMPETENCY EDUCATION

Let's examine some dimensions to think about when shifting the cultures for teaching and learning through the lens of educational leadership. In my experience, seven dimensions of leadership need to be attended to if a transition to CBE is to be successful, as depicted in figure 8.1.

Vision Building

Building a vision for the future of education in a school or district is a community-based process. Once fashioned, the vision must be held, nurtured, and integrated throughout all functions within the governance of the school or district. If a district has several schools, each having its own vision or mission statement, the statements should align with the district vision.

FIGURE 8.1   Dimensions of leadership in competency-based education

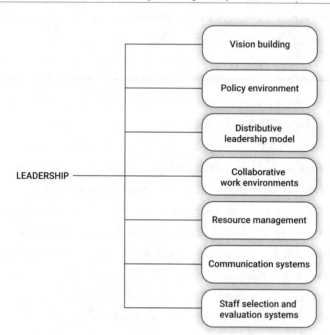

The role of leadership is to make sure that the vision serves as the foundation of the transformation and is never reduced to that forgotten mission statement on the wall near the school entrance. It should be part of the day-to-day decision making. This idea is similar to Grant Wiggins and Jay McTighe's notion of mission integration in their book *Schooling by Design*.[2] Central office and school-based leaders must challenge each other when making annual budget decisions to ensure that every decision moves the school or district forward toward the vision. School boards and committees must likewise use that same lens when approving budgets. As leaders, we have to challenge political candidates who wish to be elected to school board and committee positions and ask them to specifically speak to how they will move the vision forward. In fact, wise leaders could invite these candidates into the schools to show them how the work going on there is connected to the vision. Too many candidates win elections by selling their personal agendas, which may not align with the school's mission. Again, political involvement is a bit of a different role for local school leaders. In many cases, we just cross our fingers and hope that pro-education candidates win favor with the electorate. If we want good outcomes, we must politically engage around our vision.

Building a vision for CBE is difficult work. Long-standing programs and some personnel positions and roles will most likely change. For teachers, job orientation and roles will also change over time. Unless leaders continually and explicitly keep the vision in front of everyone's thinking, the reasons for making changes will be forgotten, perhaps opening up channels of resistance that were not there at the beginning. Sometimes it helps to create a logo or catchphrase for the vision to quickly focus conversations.

An important part of leadership in this regard is to keep a laser-like focus on the steps the district feels are the priority in launching and moving this work. Prioritizing is often problematic for administrative teams. As leaders, we believe that *everything* is important and we can't drop any balls. I have used a helpful exercise with my own faculty when we were faced with initiative overload. I had all my teachers list all the items on their plates when they come to work. We literally filled a whiteboard with programs, meetings, and other activities and duties. I wasn't even aware of some things the teachers felt they had to do because they were charged to do those things by a previous principal. I simply was unaware of the burden of that responsibility on them. A group of volunteers then took all the items and culled them down to a short list of the items most important in improving student learning. This list was brought back to the faculty for further discussion. As the school principal, I felt it helped all of us come to a common understanding of what was most important and allowed us not to feel guilty about removing items that had the least bearing on student learning.

Having a leadership team identify all the initiatives and activities across the district is an important exercise. I have found that members of some teams don't even know what other members do in the full spectrum of their responsibilities. From their whiteboard filled with activities and programs, they can then select the items that will be most important in moving toward CBE. This type of focus also safeguards the district from jumping into any more initiatives or interesting conferences, programs, or expenses that are not in keeping with the consensus on what is essential to the vision. As we will see, this activity also helps in reorganizing governance and roles within the leadership team and educator roles.

Policy Environment

It is our responsibility as leaders to be sure that what we are asking of our teachers has the sanctioning of both state and local policy. For this reason, in moving past the vision, we need to think through the impact that changes may have on the day-to-day operation of the schools and on teaching and learning.

State policy may sometimes be unforgiving, yet many states currently have policies or the ability to waive policy under certain circumstances, so that schools can move toward CBE. For example, in New Hampshire, state regulations formerly required 180 days of school each year. One policy change that enabled a great deal of innovation in structuring the school day and year came with a change of language that requires elementary, middle, and high schools to meet a specified number of hours, not days, each year. This level of flexibility creates some innovation space for how time can be used to support the learning outcomes of the district. However, it is only innovative if people take advantage of what this type of policy language can do. Professional organizations within a state can also be helpful resources in influencing the direction that state policy is framed. This type of organic or grassroots push to change policy shouldn't be overlooked when existing state policy is limited in allowing changes in school practices.

At the local level, teachers often confuse policy with practice. When a certain practice is in place for a long time, people often just assume that it is district policy. Sometimes, great ideas are squashed because it is assumed that school policy won't allow them, even though it isn't explicitly stated. Perhaps a local policy still requires a Carnegie unit specifying the number of hours per credit, but the language is not explicit in requiring it to be in face-to-face instruction. This situation could open up possibilities for extended learning opportunities (ELOs) in the community just by thoughtful interpretation of existing policy. Thus, state and local policies may sometimes be a boost or a barrier to the design of CBE.

Distributive Leadership Model

Moving to CBE within a district can't be owned by only one leader. Many of us can remember having to jump onto a new initiative pushed by an incoming superintendent and then simply jumping out of the work when the superintendent left the district. To do the work of CBE, one single person can't own and direct the work in top-down fashion; we have to adopt a distributive model of leadership. CBE does not lend itself to sending teachers out for training to come back and implement. This is not work that we plan for a year and put into full implementation. In designing CBE, we ask shareholders to cocreate, design, build, and test the work in small measures. With that experience, they can take their work and further develop it, try something different, or reject it. This is a new role for teachers and administrators. In this new environment of designing better teaching and learning systems, we put our people in the drivers' seat of the work they want to do, giving them full latitude to bring their creativity and innovation into their thinking while giving them the time and space to collaborate. They essentially become the leaders by virtue of our giving them the power of decision making in matters that move their learning designs into actionable steps in their classrooms.

For example, control of time and resources can be the role of professional learning communities. In visiting many competency-based learning environments, I have witnessed the development of powerful teaching teams whose work is collaborative and very innovative. Those teaching teams are supported by school leaders who advise and support. The degree to which distributive leadership guides school operations can result in a redefinition of school roles and responsibilities.

Pittsfield Middle High School in the Pittsfield, New Hampshire, School District has been a national model for rethinking school roles and responsibilities in its evolution to highly personalized CBE. It epitomizes a distributive leadership model by empowering the students, teachers, and parents in all facets of school planning and operations. Part of its logic model in doing this work was to rethink the adult roles.[3] Guided by expertise from the Center for Secondary School Redesign, the school made one remarkable change in roles: it dissolved the role of school principal. Essentially, the role of the principal was networked within the team through a redefinition of the school leader (administrator) roles and responsibilities and the role of the Community Advisory Council. Students have a large voice and decision-making powers on this council, while school administrators act in an advisory capacity. Although Pittsfield is a very small rural district, there are big lessons to be learned in innovation for personalized CBE. Visit the district's website (www.pittsfieldnhschools.org) to learn the history of the school's redesign.

Collaborative Work Environments

When schools are transforming to personalized learning environments, very few decisions are made by a single person. To that end, as leaders, we need to put the right people in the room at the same time. This is a challenge, as many demands of teaching isolate our professionals. Time can be our greatest asset or our greatest liability. We will never have enough additional time to do the design and implementation work that transformation requires over a period of years. Therefore, we have to use our time differently, make it part of our school day, and create collaborative work environments.

If we are asking our teachers to research, design, build prototypes, and study results, then we should be asking them to do this planning work during the school day, as part of their professional learning communities. It may take several years of schedule development to have fully functioning professional learning communities meeting regularly during the school day, but that should be the goal. In one elementary school I have worked with, the principal and assistant principal hold a multigrade gathering one day a week so that teachers can meet in vertical teams. The principals aim to embed this meeting time into the schedule permanently and expand it to a daily model.

To develop efficient and effective use of the time resources, we must first scrutinize how time is spent within a current schedule. In 2016, I was trying to solve the time dilemma with a principal who was trying to find extra time to work on developing competencies. My first question to him was, how were he and his staff currently spending their professional time? The only answer I received was that teachers met in their professional learning communities (PLCs). When further probed about what teachers did in their PLCs, the principal had no answer. It seemed that nothing very productive came out of the PLCs, because the staff had little idea about what to do during this time. This was an excellent opportunity to open up time during the day, as well as begin to develop high-functioning PLCs that have the potential to truly change the professional culture within a school.

Jonathan Vander Els, the former principal of Memorial School in the Sanborn Regional District, is a national voice on the role of PLCs in developing CBE. In "Voices from the Field: Powerful Professional Learning Communities," he describes how PLCs grew within his school.

VOICES FROM THE FIELD

POWERFUL PROFESSIONAL LEARNING COMMUNITIES

By Jonathan Vander Els, Former Principal, Memorial School, New Hampshire, and Executive Director, New Hampshire Learning Initiative

Eight years ago, our school did not set out to become a competency-based system. Rather, we recognized the need to change because not all of our students were making the progress that we wanted or expected. We eventually realized that our efforts to provide support for each of our students was very much in line with a competency-based education (CBE) approach. And the foundation for the transformation to CBE in our school started (and flourished) through our development of highly functioning professional learning communities (PLCs).

At Memorial School, we applied the four critical questions of a PLC to guide our work. Throughout our journey, these four questions assisted us in ensuring that we were providing appropriate and meaningful opportunities for all our students to demonstrate competency and progress in their learning.

What do we expect our students to learn?

We began to work very hard at clearly and precisely describing what we expected our students to know and be able to demonstrate. Our competencies were developed by teacher teams that had been working with essential standards and began to apply the even larger grain of competencies as the transferable learning.

Our teachers' increased understanding of competencies ensured a viable, successful curriculum. Our district had developed high-leverage competencies that guided the learning for students. Underneath the umbrella of the competencies and within the assessment itself, teachers identify the leverage standards that would be considered. And it did not vary from teacher to teacher within a grade level. The competencies were developed together, and the learning experiences in the classrooms were specific to those competencies.

How will we know when students have learned it?

Common summative performance assessments are a true measure of a student's competency. By design, they require a student to demonstrate and transfer learning in and across subject areas. The learning our teachers experienced through their collaborative teams specific to assessment was a monumental shift within our system. The assessment literacy of our staff increased significantly, thanks to the collaborative development performance assessments. Common summative performance assessments are the vehicle to truly capture students' understanding at a competency level, and the collaborative team is the vehicle for developing, validating, and refining these assessments. Team-created common assessments allow teams of teachers to gather data specific to each student's progression of learning. This information is then collaboratively analyzed to inform the next instructional steps and learning pathways for each student.

How will we respond when some students do not learn?

Addressing deficiencies is imperative within any educational system committed to learning for all. Our school and district integrated multiple tiers of support for all learners throughout our system. For a student to *not* learn foundational knowledge was not an option in our system. We committed to providing the time and resources within our daily schedule to ensure that all students were demonstrating their learning at the highest levels possible.

The schedules in each school allowed for students to receive additional instruction or support, depending on each student's particular needs. The extra help occurred each school day during a tier 2 time (i.e., small-group instruction). The leadership team within our school developed this schedules collaboratively to maximize any existing resources so that we could take advantage of small-group instruction (in some cases, only one or two students in a group).

This additional support is above and beyond what all students receive during tier 1, for which we ensured access to *every* student. No student was allowed to be pulled out during tier 1 instruction. Students who required even more support (a much smaller percentage) received tier 3 (whole-group) instruction as well.

How will we extend and enrich the learning for students who have demonstrated proficiency?

A CBE system lends itself very well to those students needing to be challenged. The same tiers that provide support provide various opportunities for extension. Students have opportunities both to demonstrate a deeper depth of knowledge (DOK level 4) and to extend their DOK through personalized experiences. In the development of our system, we recognized the importance of meeting each student where he or she was and affording students the opportunity and the support to continue along their own learning progression.

A majority of the behind-the-scenes work in a CBE system is accomplished during collaborative team meetings. Teams must identify the competencies and anchor the standards that are going to be assessed in their units of study. They must build performance assessments that truly assess these competencies and vet these performance assessments for quality assurance.

After reviewing and assessing student work together, the teams must then revise and refine the assessment accordingly. In addition, teams of teachers must provide reteaching and ELOs, depending on the assessment results. All these activities must be coordinated within the teams to ensure that students are receiving what they need. Highly functioning PLCs are imperative for this work to occur at peak levels, but the result is a team of educators committed to the learning of each student in the school.

———————

Collaborative work environments that are supported and coached by administrators build trust between teachers and administrators and empower teachers as decision makers. Teachers have been so hammered by the constraints of teacher evaluation systems, they often don't dare to take steps to innovate in their classrooms, because the teacher evaluations may not be complementary or supportive of the new model for teaching and learning. This is where bold leadership has to be in play. A principal has to give 360-degree support when empowering teacher leadership. If teachers take the lead to innovate in their classrooms, it is the responsibility of those in leadership to provide the support of time, financial resources, space, and systems support such as evaluation criteria to do this work.

Building collaborative work environments must be modeled by administrative teams. As leaders, we especially need to model good teamwork if we are expecting our staff to do so also. Having protocol-driven administrative team meetings can make the difference between a productive, proactive team and a simply reactive one. Many administrators move up the ranks from various school roles, but they may not be well versed in effective classroom teaching and learning strategies. The cooperative learning environment in an administrative PLC can be worthwhile to develop and hone skills in classroom observation for all members of a leadership team when they share and review teacher work.

Resource Management

Some schools and districts are very fortunate in acquiring funding through different types of innovation grants to underwrite the transition, especially in the beginning stages, to CBE. It is an important role of schools or districts to seek out funding opportunities from their state department of education, grants from local community organizations or national educational nonprofits, and, most importantly, resources that may exist within their own budget.

Time management as a resource can't be undervalued. Creatively using time differently than how it was apportioned for traditional learning can be a big breakthrough. For example, to support students in ELOs and students using alternate pathways to graduation, one school has a late start for teachers so that they are available to confer with students late in the afternoon, beyond the contracted teacher time. Working with school boards and committees to redefine what can be ordered in textbook budget lines can have a big impact on the ability to move to blended learning, giving students additional options for their learning pathways.

Our teacher resources are currently deployed using the one-teacher-per-class model. When students move at their own pace, especially when supported in blended learning in dynamic small groups, teachers may have better opportunities to actively engage with students in their performance tasks, rather than being tied up in direct instruction, class after class.

We often overlook space as a resource, but it can be a critical component of school change. If we are teaching and learning differently, we may need a different kind of space. Although we don't want to think about negative aspects of the era of the open classroom, learners using personal technology don't have to use their technology while sitting at a desk. In fact, the more usable the space is for students to find their own comfortable position, the more engaged students feel. They then can exercise choice in their learning. For a traditional school with lots of individual student desks, it may be important to replace furniture with a varied assortment of furniture possibilities.

When students are involved in resource management, good things can happen. At Parish Episcopal School in Dallas, for example, a class of math students was given a budget of ten thousand dollars to redesign its learning space. This incredibly engaging learning activity required the students to design and budget for the space, as well as do all the research and speak with contractors. The students chose to have movable table-desk units with a large whiteboard that could be flipped up for group work or arranged to create carrels for individual students. One area in the space for project work had a video station. The back of the room had a long, high table for students to stand and work, with lots of charging stations available for both handheld and mobile media. Deciding that there wasn't enough storage space for math manipulatives and equipment, the students dedicated some space for a large storage unit with transparent plastic bins. The unit was on wheels so that it could move around the room as groups needed it. The teacher's desk was an L-shaped unit with the shorter area for the teacher's personal work space and the longer part designed as an erasable whiteboard surface for the teacher to better work with the students. In a school in Colorado, a group of teachers challenged their students to find a better use of space in their old building for students to have a comfortable drop-in space for teachers and students to work together. The result was that students recaptured poorly used spaces such as the ends of hallways. These spaces allowed the students to remain closer to their classrooms and teachers instead of having to go to the school's other designated work spaces.

Projects like these underscore the importance of involving students in the design of their space. The more ownership they have in their school, the more pride they will have in their learning. These opportunities for student agency also move beyond academics into the day-to-day world of their school's operations and many of the processes that they will work with in their chosen workplace.

Communication Systems

School transformation over time requires a special focus on effective communication. For this reason, school leaders can't only think about how they are communicating with parents about their children's school. Effective communication is really a two-way street. It isn't enough for us to think that writing a column in a community newspaper or a school letter is effective in reaching an intended audience or even believing that everyone will read it and act on the information.

As a principal, I was often confronted by teachers who were frustrated with parents who were unaware of the expectations of the class. When asked, the teachers generally said they explained the rules and expectations at open house and reminded parents in emails. The reality is, not all parents attend open houses, and they are often overwhelmed by educational jargon and the unfamiliarity with the teachers standing before them. The challenge in communicating such information is to be sure that teachers forge relationships with parents through phone calls, emails, text messaging, teacher websites, and newsletters and invite parents into their classrooms and exhibitions of learning.

Effective communication is important. It is a two-way process with which we must prioritize what is most important for our communities to know about teaching and learning. Grounding this in the vision work and reminding parents about the purpose of the work is essential. In essence, we have to learn how to brand our work in much the same way that a product brand conjures up mental images as soon as we see it. At school budget time, we begin pleading with parents to attend meetings that decide budgets, but we often have not effectively communicated why we are asking for funding from the public. In many cases, those who are voting on our budgets have no direct connection to our schools, so why would they vote in favor of something that would raise their taxes? As education leaders, we must create far more effective means of communicating with the public, not just the parents, as we move traditional teaching and learning to CBE. It does take a system of communication that should be intentionally built with great clarity within a school or district.

Staff Selection and Evaluation Systems

As schools begin to transform, it becomes important to select the right people to move the organization into the future. Note the difference between hiring staff and selecting staff. The traditional approach of reviewing résumés of prospective teacher candidates to come in for an interview is simply inadequate for developing CBE. You need to select staff members who have a growth mind-set, the ability to learn by doing, digital literacy skills, and the ability both to collaborate and to lead. You will most likely be able to elaborate on these skills according to your own set of needs as you build the profile of a teacher in your school of the future. We can do much better than cherry-picking through a pile of résumés in the hopes of picking a good one. In this area, we should look to other industries that hire key personnel.

I often tell my advanced graduate studies students that they must hire as if they were a *Fortune* 500 company. What does that mean? Running ads in the paper or posting openings is a great way to attract a lot of applicants but maybe not the right ones. The challenge in selecting staff is to market yourselves to attract the right candidates. Do you have some really great teachers in your school? Go to them, and personally ask them if any of their contacts would think about applying to teach in your school—network, network, network! Contact your local college or university teacher education programs. Ask them if you can contact their best and brightest student teaching candidates. There can be many creative strategies in marketing. One rural school in a hard-to-hire area offers full-season ski passes as part of the benefits package. Begin to survey Twitter feeds and LinkedIn to make further contacts. You may have fewer applications, but they may be a better field of candidates to consider.

Much as a large company provides a prospectus on who it is, a school district should prepare an attractive prospectus of the school to share information about the community history, the social and cultural life, and the political and economic characteristics of the school's location—generally a good immersion into the life of the school community. Then, with a focus on the school, you can bring the applicant into the school's vision, its hopes for the future, what the vision of the graduate actually means in the teaching and learning that goes on each day. This type of prospectus can be easily digitized as a magazine with embedded short videos. In other words, we must begin selling our schools and inviting prospective applicants to apply knowing that the school is moving forward with new designs in teaching and learning.

The next recommendation for staff selection may go against the grain of tradition. Why wait for a candidate to come in to answer questions blindly? Prepare five to eight questions that probe the candidate's readiness for the job, using the profile you have built for a high-quality teacher. Ask teacher candidates to submit their responses so that the field of candidates for interview can be chosen. From the submitted applications, conduct a phone interview with each promising candidate, and telephone their references. When you have chosen your candidates for an in-person interview, ask him or her to provide a digital portfolio that speaks to the areas the school has prioritized for moving forward. Be very clear about the profile you have built to find a teacher for your school. You will not find the perfect person, but you will find candidates who have a higher chance of success with you. This may sound like a great deal of work. It is. However, following these recommendations will help you learn far more about the potential of your selected candidate to work in the professional culture of your school.

Once teachers are selected, schools and districts must align their teacher evaluation system with their expectations. One frustration that I often hear from teachers is that if they try to do some new things in their classroom, they fear they will get dinged on their evaluations because their observable teaching behaviors do not match the criteria in the evaluation model. Most evaluation systems are built on the face-to-face, one-size-fits-all model, with a nod to some differentiation practices during the lesson. If you have an expectation that teachers work in powerful PLCs to develop responsive, personalized teaching, how does your evaluation system support, encourage, and coach teachers in this model? How is PLC work evaluated as part of a teacher evaluation system? It would help if CBE leaders in a school or district sat down to create a learning progression of teacher behaviors that they could frequently observe in classrooms over a long period.

Ongoing, frequent feedback is the fuel for professional growth. We need to build systems of support and evaluation that fit this new model. This doesn't mean that we walk away from research-based teacher evaluation models. We must use them in different ways and at different times. The Sanborn School District suspended its teacher evaluations for one year while administrators learned how to best support and evaluate teachers in their new CBE system. They didn't want teachers to suffer in any way while they were learning about new ways to evaluate teachers in the classroom. Teachers were relieved and incredibly engaged in working with the feedback they received, and they gave great feedback to the administrators to further improve the evaluation criteria.

Mary Heath, former deputy commissioner of education in New Hampshire and the former assistant superintendent in the school district I once worked, shared an important perspective with me that I have never forgotten. She said that we shouldn't be so preoccupied with teachers who can't do the work we ask of them when 99 percent of the teachers are good teachers who do their best each day. Basically, Sanborn used this thinking when it suspended its teacher evaluation program for a year. District leaders knew that if they had a teacher who needed to improve or be considered for nonrenewal, they could move forward with the necessary actions. For the 99 percent of the teachers who were working hard every day moving the district forward in their vision, the Sanborn administrators needed and wanted their feedback as part of piloting their new evaluation system.

The challenges of connecting the dots of systemic change and growth toward CBE are complex. However, as leaders, the more we do to connect the work across the teaching and learning spectrum in coherent ways, the fewer barriers emerge in moving the work forward.

THE LEADERS' CBE TOOLKIT

Where does a school leader begin in the quest to move to CBE? We currently have no graduate programs to prepare us. Principal and superintendent certification programs may not even touch on the new innovations in competency-based teaching and learning. Simply visiting schools that are doing this work will not provide the broad and deep understanding for CBE.

The chapter appendix is a compendium of resources that I found are most helpful for school leaders who need to better understand CBE. The resources mentioned in the appendix represent only a few of the many resources available nationally to support your efforts to develop personalized CBE. How would you use these tools? In the next chapter, let's examine two case studies of school districts that chose to transform their schools to CBE.

Appendix (Chapter 8)

Resources in Competency Education for School Leaders in Competency-Based Education

CompetencyWorks (www.competencyworks.org): The national resource for CBE provides any researched-based briefing papers, daily blogs by practitioners, a wiki on national policy and practice, case studies, and other up-to-date information. Chris Sturgis of MetisNet directs CompetencyWorks and is a leading national expert on CBE.

iNACOL (International Association for K–12 Online Learning) (www.inacol.org): This group is the parent organization of CompetencyWorks. Susan Patrick, executive director of iNACOL, is an international expert in competency-based blended and online learning. The annual fall convening of iNACOL's Blended and Online Learning symposium, with an expansive strand of CBE sessions, brings thousands of educators together to learn from each other. iNACOL works diligently to develop K–12 education policy in support of advancing transformational models of teaching and learning in competency-based, blended and online learning environments.

So You Think You Want to Innovate? (http://learningaccelerator.org/so-you-think -you-want-to-innovate): This tool, developed by Learning Accelerator and 2Revolutions, is best used by a school or district's administrative team. The leadership and communications sections are especially strong for administrative team goal setting. Other sections of the tool include resource allocation, structure and process, capacity, policy environment, and learning agenda. I often recommend this tool as a first step in leadership work in designing future models for teaching and learning.

2Revolutions (www.2Revolutions.net): This education design lab provides support services to education using integrative design principles. It works with educators to approach complex problems as design thinkers to identify root causes, design solutions at the right scale, and clarify testable hypotheses. The design lab helps national policy makers, state organizations, and school districts transform teaching and learning. Its *Future of Learning* video is a powerful way for staff to begin thinking about new designs for learning.

Robert J. Marzano, Phil Warrick, and Julia A. Simms, *A Handbook for High Reliability Schools* (Bloomington, IN: Solution Tree, 2014): This text is a rich resource of research-based practices and methods in support of school reform. According to this book, the schools with the highest level of reliability practice CBE. As a handbook, it offers many tools such as surveys and assessments for schools to build their own reality check on where they are with respect to school reform.

Next Generation Learning Challenge (http://nextgenlearning.org): This organization offers learning-challenge grants to redesign new learning systems. In addition to grant opportunities, the organization offers many resources on its website to help educators think through transformational designs.

Digital Promise (http://digitalpromise.org): This organization supports learning in new and different ways through the power of technology and collaboration through its League of Innovative Schools. Digital Promise has been at the forefront of many national conversations in school transformation.

Education Elements (www.edelements.com): This consulting group, founded by Anthony Kim, provides a range of services for schools moving toward personalized, blended learning models. A helpful resource for download is EdElements Personalized Learning Playbook.

Achieve (www.achieve.org): As an organization, Achieve is committed to supporting the effort to prepare all students for college and career readiness, both at the policy and the implementation levels. Achieve's Community Based Pathways Communications Toolkit and resources on competency-based transcripts, learning progressions, innovation zones, and various webinars should be in every school leader's toolkit.

Getting Smart (http://gettingsmart.com): This enterprise by Tom VanderArk supports educational technology, blended learning, leadership, and learning. Its website is filled with resources that include blogs and other publications, leadership initiatives, and up-to-date information on schools across the country.

Education Reimagined (http://education-reimagined.org): This organization has a vision of the transformation of school-centered to student-centered learning. Its transformational vision document can be the starting point for any school or district beginning this work. The website also offers extensive profiles of schools that have evolved into highly personalized, competency-based, learner-centric environments.

Center for Secondary School Redesign (http://cssr.us): The center offers a wide range of resources and services in support of redesigning personalized secondary schools. Joe DiMartino, founder of CSSR, is a national expert in personalization. He and his team have managed multiple national innovation grants across many schools. The leadership tools are especially helpful for administrative teams. All materials are available on the center's website.

Todd Rose, *The End of Average: How We Succeed in a World That Values Sameness* (New York: HarperOne, 2016): This book should be read, digested, and discussed by educators. It can provide some rich thinking for leaders designing personalized CBE. Todd Rose provides sound reasoning for considering that the "average" is used erroneously throughout our society. He outlines recommendations for education to more purposefully and soundly communicate student learning by including competency education.

Richard DeLorenzo et al., *Delivering on the Promise: The Education Revolution* (Bloomington, IN: Solution Tree, 2008): This book is a must-read for anyone taking a deep dive into shifting school architecture to CBE. This insightful, honest book drives the importance of building the new architecture of professional work beyond the boundaries that have shackled us to the traditional systems of learning of past generations.

Chapter 9

The Architectural Shifts: Case Studies

EDUCATION HAS RELIED on the unchanging nature of how we educate our children and operate our schools. For generation upon generation, the same thing has been happening in the same way in our schools, with only few major shifts in some of these routines. The length of the school day and year, the organization of how students learn during the day, the academic offerings, how teachers are organized and work within the school, and how we finance our school operations—all have been routinized into a structure and pace we are all familiar with and have found comfort in within our communities. Essentially, the building blocks of the architecture of our schools have remained the same for decades.

What would cause us to upset these building blocks or shift them around? This is a fundamental question we ask about the shift from traditional teaching and learning to CBE. For many schools, during the NCLB era of high-stakes testing, a few of the blocks that were crumbling in our structure were reexamined and fixed. Much of the data mining during that time revealed that traditional education was leaving many children behind. For many schools, the fixes were only temporary, and for other schools, many fixes just didn't work to repair the deeper, structural problems. This analogy speaks to the difference between efforts to reform and efforts to transform. *Reform* may only shift blocks around or reshape or fix some blocks. *Transform* means to change the structure substantially into something that may only resemble the original shape or form.

Transformation is a systemic architectural shift. In examining the architectural framework of competency education through the lens of competency development, performance assessment, personalized pathways, grading, and leadership, you might come away rather overwhelmed. Where to begin transforming a school organization that delivers on the promise made with a community to work toward a vision of college and career readiness?

In chapter 8, you could examine resources that included profiles of schools that have been making this transformation for many years. This chapter offers an in-depth look at the journeys of two school districts toward CBE. These two stories have a lot to teach us about transforming K–12 systems of learning.

CHUGACH, ALASKA, SCHOOL DISTRICT

The first story is about the quest of the Chugach School District to create proficiency-based, personalized learning. I first learned of this effort in 2011 at a convening of early CBE pioneers—organizations, schools, and state organizations that were developing competency-based, personalized learning systems. The school leaders from Chugach described how they essentially had gone through so many school improvement struggles that they needed to reexamine their past efforts, considering their low student performance data. Despite purchasing a new reading program to raise student reading scores, they were faltering in their efforts.

Chris Sturgis of CompetencyWorks has written about her insights from an extensive visit to Chugach.[1] The synopsis below is meant to capture the essence of Chugach's journey based on Sturgis's reporting. As you think through Chugach's developmental process, begin thinking about where you are in your journey and how Chugach's story may help you to begin telling yours.

Chugach, a very small, rural Alaskan school district with an enrollment of 370 students in five schools, was created in 1975 to deeply improve education in Alaska Native communities and in response to increased public funding made available through the expansion of the oil industry. After more than fifteen years, the Chugach community was still dismayed with the low achievement levels of their students. In search of the reasons for this, Chugach began a period of self-examination. Issues of trust in schools and with educators had a cultural basis, while district leaders had to acknowledge that they weren't reaching all students successfully. As late as 1992–1993, student performance on state tests in language arts and math showed that the district's students were performing at less than 25 percent proficiency.

The school district's attempt to raise reading scores with a new program didn't work. District leaders needed to probe deeper into the culture for teaching and learning as well as the culture within their community to discover who they were as a school district. They had to know their own identity before they could establish a vision for the future.

Through Chugach's development of its mission and strategic planning, the district kept students at the center. It was clear that the leadership wanted the students to have a vested interest and ownership in their learning to be best prepared for their adult roles. The district felt a need to honor the students' cultural heritage by creating experiential learning opportunities that were based in the community and engaged the community members directly in the children's learning.

The educational leaders were very clear about the values that supported their emerging model of personalized learning. Each school in the district took on this set of values and further customized it to the local school cultures. The forward direction of the schools' missions and their work had shared purpose.

Students and faculty embraced the notion that they were all learners in this process. That meant that things could be messy and that some learning would come from mistakes, whether they were by children or adults. The design cycle that Chugach used involved planning, implementing, evaluating, and refining. Because this was a cycle of continuous improvement, it created a culture that embraced a growth mind-set both in students and in staff members. Students could experience growth over time by developing their own personal learning plans, which also developed career goals, a community-based value.

With the recognition that early efforts to improve student proficiency floundered, Chugach used its laser focus to bring *each* student to a defined basic skills proficiency while recognizing that the learning must be developmentally appropriate if it were to engage each student. While district leaders made their core beliefs in character education central to the design of learning opportunities for students, they also valued real-world learning to help the students make the transition from school to life. They also decided early on to provide technology both as an educational tool and as a tool they would need to use later in life.

The only way Chugach could think through meeting individual student needs was to think differently about how students had to engage personally in where they were on their personal learning continuum. They arranged their curriculum into domains that had associated levels with clear performance indicators on which students were assessed. This framework allowed students to move forward at their own pace toward their graduation requirements. The combination of this curriculum design and having students move toward their graduation goals at their own pace meant that their personal skills development was also a part of their progress toward graduation. The goal setting and self-reflection in their personal learning plans set the stage for continual growth and development.

Chugach also adopted a simple, common grading assessment for all scoring. The district defined its benchmarks for proficiency at 80 percent. However, no one single assessment determines proficiency. Chugach uses a broader and varied assessment strategy that begins with a student's own assessment of his or her learning. From there, scores from both a skills assessment and a performance assessment are used to determine if a student has met proficiency and is ready for the next level of learning. Such a system requires a great deal of teacher-student communication and flexibility while learning is taking place. The experiential nature of Chugach students' learning takes them outside the classroom as well. In Chugach, these learning experiences are grounded in the local culture. Teachers use their expertise and professional judgment to accommodate learning and assessments as needed for students.

Like the Pittsfield, New Hampshire, School District, Chugach began its work with a sense of oneness with the community. The schools were not just located on a street in the community; the school *is* the community, and the community *is* the school. Building strong bonds through learning and growing together built the trust and transparency that the schools needed to move forward in their work. Because of this like-mindedness, the school board was well on board with the school's mission and strategic plan.

One resource that Chugach used extensively in this journey was the Re-inventing Schools Coalition. The systemic support of this coalition guided the work in developing Chugach's proficiency-based, personalized learning model. The coalition, now known as Reinventing Schools (rs.marzanoresearch.com), partners with many districts in supporting district, school, and teacher development.

While Chugach is somewhat of a poster child for a twenty-year profile in developing CBE, we always come back to this question: is it working? Be mindful that the metric for success must be based on the chosen focus of the work that catapulted a school or district into the redesign. For Chugach, the focus was literacy. In 1992, Chugach's reading proficiency was less than 25 percent on the state test. In 2013–2014, after twenty years of moving toward student-centered, tech-enabled, proficiency-based education, the Chugach schools' literacy rate rose to 80 percent.[2] Although this metric is convincing, the most important results of Chugach's transformation represent far more than test scores.

This is another shift to consider when you tell the public about your own school's transformation. NCLB forced us to think about test scores as a measure of school improvement, but test scores can and should only be part of the metrics used in measuring our progress toward student-centered, personalized learning. Go back to your vision statement. What are the metrics you will be tracking? This is what your community needs to hear about. Some of those metrics may be qualitative as well as quantitative.

Chugach's story is amazing. Its example can speak to you in your developmental work as you build your new architecture and contemplate your shifts to CBE. However, you may begin second-guessing yourself with "yes, but" thoughts. Your journey will most likely be different from Chugach's, with different metrics to guide you along the way. As the focus of your work gains clarity, recognize your boosts and your barriers. What are you doing now that works well on all levels and is critical to moving forward? What are the barriers to meeting your vision? Think carefully through your barriers, and be honest about what they are. For each barrier, decide how you can remove or work around it, and recognize if you have an insurmountable barrier. A barrier may cause you to redirect some of your efforts or make a monumental change at some point in the process. One such barrier that may erupt in a long-range plan can be demographics. With enrollment declining because of demographic changes, you may have to fundamentally shift at a time when this shift will be very disruptive. When, and if, this happens, you may need to readjust your design for the future in keeping with your vision.

Because Chugach is a small, rural district in Alaska, it may be difficult for you to see how you can parallel this small district's work in your own district if it is suburban or urban. For this reason, let's look at a larger public school district whose path of redesign over the past nine years has catapulted it to national prominence.

SANBORN REGIONAL SCHOOL DISTRICT

The Sanborn Regional School District is in the southeastern region of New Hampshire, approximately one hour north of Boston. In 2016–2017, the district pupil enrollment was 1,665, with a professional staff of 158. The district has four schools: D.J. Bakie School (preK–5), located in Kingston; Memorial School (preK–5), located in Newton; Sanborn Regional Middle School, located in Newton; and Sanborn Regional High School, located in Kingston and serving the communities of Kingston, Newton, and Fremont.

Before 2007, the Sanborn Regional School District had experienced quite a bit of upheaval. There had been a stream of short-term superintendents and other school leadership. The high school facilities were in great disrepair, compromising the school's ability to pass regional accreditation. Overcoming many barriers, the community moved forward in building the current Sanborn Regional High School, which opened in 2006.

In 2008, Brian Blake, the newly appointed superintendent, contacted me to meet with him and Ellen Hume-Howard, the district's curriculum director. Blake and I had worked together in the Goffstown School District, and I also had the pleasure of working with him on the School Administrators Leading with Technology Gates Grant when he was a superintendent in Farmington, New Hampshire. During that first meeting in Sanborn, I forged a relationship with the district's leaders and teachers—a relationship that has grown for eight years through the entire evolution of the district to CBE. In the initial stages of the work, there was no intention to move to CBE as a firm target for this work. However, it was clear that Blake and his team wanted to pull the district out of its past to become a high performing district. Competency development was definitely on the radar screen, and the high school needed to address this quickly, as it was facing the state mandate to have those in place by 2008 to be in compliance with the New Hampshire's Minimum Standards for School Approval.

One thing you learn when working with the Sanborn team is that everything it does is informed by educational research. The first piece of work was very revealing. If the team members wanted to have a high-functioning, effective school, then they needed to research exactly what an effective school means and collect data from within to determine how effective they were. They used Lawrence Lezotte's correlates of effective schools to guide their data gathering.[3] Their laser-like focus in the early days of district transformation was a bit like the Little Engine That Could. After examining their data against the correlates, they focused on working hard at being in the top 10 percent of schools in the state. The top 10 percent of what? you might ask. Their answer was equally simple: everything. They developed district goals that included integration of technology in instruction, grouping strategies and differentiation to address what they had discovered in their data mining. Through this work, the administrative team members, who were all relatively new to their positions, forged a working bond rarely seen in collaborative administrative teams. Their leadership qualities individually and as a team are remarkable. For this reason, this team has stayed intact and worked together since 2008, although one member, Jonathan Vander Els, has since moved on to direct a state-level organization, the New Hampshire Learning Initiative.

In was in the first two years that competency development took place at the middle school and high school. The team devoted several professional days to school-level teams and grades 6–12 vertical team collaboration to arrive at the content-area competencies. The work progressed well, but it also uncovered some curriculum area weaknesses. The middle school science program required quite a bit of development work, and then there was a need to articulate that work with the high school science program. Hume-Howard is a literacy and assessment specialist and has an in-depth understanding of the Common Core State Standards in ELA. Donna Donnell, the mathematics coordinator, likewise has a deep understanding of these standards in mathematics and the standards' linkages to the schools' mathematics program, Everyday Mathematics. Both women worked diligently at helping the faculty better understand the Common Core under a lens of assessment.

This initial work in deconstructing the standards allowed the team to focus on the bigger ideas of the curriculum. In those first two years, competencies were not addressed for kindergarten through grade 6. The team only considered alignment to Common Core State Standards and the development of power standards (essential standards) mapped onto the units of instruction. They were better able to focus on creating learning expectations for different periods during the school year by doing this work. My role with the district was to provide large- and small-group support and coaching for competency development, to develop the science competencies and curriculum at the secondary level, to support the development of performance-based assessment practices, to coach the administrative team, and to give guidance in the shaping of the teacher evaluation system.

Launching the Work

By 2009–2010, the work had taken on greater focus. The district had purchased a new student information system. Part of that system was the grade book software Pinnacle. It was relatively easy to load the competencies for grades 9–12 into the grade book to effectively begin the competency-based grading. However, the grade book for K–6, loaded with standards, seemed quite foreign to the staff. Elementary teachers had some difficulty connecting the work that students were doing with how the assessments were entered into the grade book. The first report card quarter was very stressful for the K–6 staff in both elementary schools. At the middle and high school level, it was easier to associate the day-to-day work to competencies. But the source of greater frustration and anxiety came with the adherence to the new grading philosophy that was incorporated into that year's faculty handbook. Slowly, over the course of that first year, the bumpy road became smoother. Administrators stood side by side with their teachers, improving the system as they went along, but also holding firm to the research-based best practices in their grading philosophy statement. The report cards that year gave parents more information than they previously had about their child's learning.

Letter and number grading carried over into the report card as the parents were accustomed to seeing these. In addition, competencies and standards further informed what the students were learning. Academic grading was separated from nonacademic factors.

One aspect of grading that required greater understanding by all parties was the concept that the new grading system created rolling grades. As described earlier in chapter 7, standards- or competency-based grading creates a bucket of grades whose overall interpretation of proficiency is not artificially determined on time-based reporting periods. Proficiency is determined over the course of time. Sanborn kept its competency-based grading open for the year, or for the course, while formally reporting at regular quarterly intervals. With the grading software, Sanborn could pilot the use of trend lines in calculating grading information for students.

During the 2009–2010 school year, there was quite a bit of development in the area of curriculum in both literacy and numeracy. New curriculum approaches included guided reading, "Key 3" note taking, Lucy Calkins's nationally recognized methods for writing, the "6 Traits" writing assessment model, and further competency development and refinement. It was in this year that the PLC work took hold throughout the district. This PLC work resulted in teachers using data to best meet the instructional needs of their students. For example, the elementary schools began their WIN/LEAP time as part of their school day. This period provided interventions using flexible grouping across grade levels. And at the middle school, a block for reteaching and enrichment (which was redefined from a previous program) began to address the needs of both struggling and advanced learners.

Deepening the Work

Over the next three years, through June 2014, Sanborn continued to drill down into its model, shaping it to better meet the needs of the students while continuing to develop stronger PLCs. As grading practices and reporting criteria became more refined and understood by teachers, the faculty was better able to communicate with parents about their child's proficiency.

The district extended the work in competency development to K–6 by simply taking the power standards identified in earlier work and putting them under an umbrella competency statement. During that period, the New Hampshire Department of Education offered quality performance assessment training to school districts statewide (see chapter 10). Sanborn's teams took part in this four-day training over the course of two years. Not all the teachers in the district could attend the training, but those who did attend emerged as leaders in developing assessment literacy across the district. The result was better alignment between academic competencies and performance assessments that were tuned to the appropriate DOK to assess student proficiency. This alignment helped anchor the staff's work, which was driven by the engine of PLCs. Because of the PLCs' effectiveness, the district maintained ongoing support for these communities, giving them dedicated time to work together and align with the district's competency design and assessment. As a result, the thriving PLCs had a synergistic effect in moving Sanborn further along in its CBE work.

In "Voices from the Field: An End to Promiscuous Professional Development," Bryan Setser and Amy Schwann of Matchbook Learning speak to the productive and powerful work that teachers engage in when administrators break through the cycle of impractical traditional professional development of teachers.

VOICES FROM THE FIELD
AN END TO PROMISCUOUS PROFESSIONAL DEVELOPMENT

By Bryan Setser and Amy Swann, Matchbook Learning

Schools are accustomed to changing—promiscuously and routinely without producing any improvement.

—RICHARD ELMORE

At Matchbook Learning, a nonprofit charter management organization, we'd like to put an end to promiscuous professional development. By promiscuous professional development, we mean demonstrating or implying an undiscriminating or unselective approach to why educators choose certain professional development topics and the indiscriminate or casual way educators often go about deciding the relative value of the experience.

In blogs and end-of-year surveys over the past five years, teachers routinely share experiences regarding poorly designed professional learning. In addition, compliance-related professional development often dominates top-down mandates from state agencies.

Recently, the emergence of Edcamps, job-embedded learning, and teacher-led professional learning all create cool and whimsical opportunities to learn a new skill, technology tool, or process that is useful in terms of anytime, anywhere learning. And yet, school leaders have a dilemma in terms of the rate of learning for adults just as they have for students.

The choices can feel endless, and the imaginative nature of professional development experiences can mimic promiscuity in a relationship. Minus a long-term commitment and with the absence of accountability, educators can often feel like they are going to a host of one-night stands instead of being a part of a long-term growth experience or relationship. These marketplace approaches lead us to a few questions about, and solutions to, how we are turning promiscuous professional development into purposeful professional learning at Matchbook. We'll address four questions that move us toward more committed professional learning relationships at Matchbook.

What does accountability mean in a long-term relationship?

We've now spent over two decades in PLC research and practice as an industry. Professionals' fidelity to one PLC fluctuates across the country as leaders cycle in and out of systems and as organizations often fail to define the "vows of a union." We hope to guide the industry through our research about commitment within a community and through our measurements of both formal and informal learning.

It is very important to be explicit about expectations up front and to clarify what is constituted as "stepping out" on the relationship by "flirting" with other vendors, courses, experiences, and nonaligned professional learning. To minimize the temptation of our school leaders and teachers to flirt with others or step out on our expectations, our model has developed clear learning outcomes, metrics to encourage performance, and opportunities to design new teaching and learning strategies.

Indeed, there are nuances around professional learning, improvement, and exposure. In seeking to codify the rate of professional learning, educators sometimes miss coaching moments among their peers and other teachable moments, where learning is happening all the time all around us with every person in the building. Discount a culture of learning in favor of only what you can measure, and educators can miss some opportunities to move the organization and the individual.

Is it more important to have an experience or a commitment?

Richard Elmore of the Harvard Graduate School of Education discusses the importance of continuity in learning: "Improvement means engagement in learning new practices that work, based on external evidence and benchmarks of success, across multiple schools and classrooms, in specific areas of academic content and pedagogy, resulting in continuous improvement of students' academic performance overtime."[4]

While choice-driven professional learning may result in a few classroom changes or a thrilling one-night webinar stand, it does not focus on changing processes or structures for scale. We're working very hard at Matchbook to align our performance improvement process with the Baldrige Framework for Excellence. We've chosen this framework for its track record of education results. In an effort to meet the standards of excellence in the seven Baldrige categories, we've launched a micro-credentialing process that is both scalable and aligned to our student learning cycle for all adult learners at Matchbook.

In our professional learning model, our staff members begin the relationship with us by going through our specialized two-week course, which is their initial commitment to the learning phases of the badging process (the progressive learning phases are a little like the merit badges earned in the Boy Scouts of America). Then after having gone through the learning, conferencing, applying, and assessment phases in ninety-day cycles throughout the year, each participant is evaluated on his or her individual strengths and gaps as they relate to our professional learning categories under the Baldrige framework.

Staff members get a voice in how the early "dating" with our model will go as they self-reflect during ninety-day reviews and on their end-of-year reviews. From these reviews and in collaboration with coaches, they begin to personalize where they need coaching and support. They also reserve the right to accelerate that process by earning badges not just in a role area like teaching, but also in areas like technology, senior leadership, or finance in coaching conferences with our team. These protocols are very much like committed relationships. They require check-ins, a demonstration of effort, empathy for struggle, and support to grow in our model and as an individual. And we do not prohibit informal learning, peer-to-peer observations, or learning with students in design cycles or challenges. We just make sure that the ninety-day cycle and the resulting teaching portfolios at least codify the journey.

Can professional development achieve individual and collective goals in a long-term relationship with Matchbook?

In many school districts across the country, teachers or principals often submit their own individual goals, school goals, and growth goals in the form of a self-reflection checklist. Moreover, courses, conferences, and workshops often populate the portfolio as well. For the individual, a strategy or tool to enhance a practice may make its way back into practice, but more often, the one-day stand provides an enthusiastic thrill for the moment, and then the participants are left without follow-through or a call back. Additionally, if they do decide to try a relationship with the idea or practice promoted in the session, it is often unclear how the time invested in the session and the strategy behind it improved the collective good of the school. It is kind of like saying, "I've dated a lot of suitors, and that has taught me what I want and don't want." The reality is we learn from every relationship and those learning moments are hard to codify.

Promiscuity alone does not lead to wisdom. Wisdom is found in an understanding of how to be emotionally available to individual growth and the collective good. The value of true transformation is also found in how one improves one's capacity to contribute to the collective good of the school or the organization. In our work at Matchbook, we are aligning capacity development areas through our badging effort and supporting how that badging pursuit affects the collective good of our academic, behavioral, satisfaction, and retention goals.

We want a committed relationship with our employees for many years to come, and we want them to try things that spice up the relationship. Attending an online course in and of itself is not wrong; learning never is. However, we want to ensure they always understand the value of a learning opportunity and the relationship between that and the collective good for Matchbook Learning. In turn, we want to reward the investment of their time for both informal and formal learning.

Should we change attitudes or practice first in moving toward committed relationships?

Catherine Miles Grant summarizes Guskey's views on whether it is more productive to change attitudes or practices: "He argues that practice changes attitudes rather than vice versa. Rather than exhorting teachers to believe that students can learn differently, or that different students can learn at higher levels, then showing teachers the practices that go with these beliefs, Guskey argues that teachers must actually try these new practices with the students . . . If the new practices succeed with those students, then teachers have the opportunity" to change their attitudes about the practice.[5]

Teachers at Matchbook do not earn badges to demonstrate a specific skill. Rather, the badge is attained only after consistent, frequent demonstration. We set ninety-day-cycle benchmarks so we can be reflective with teachers about what they are learning. We want them to see other teachers in practice and reflect on what they saw through video and classroom observation. In true Guskey fashion, the next step is to practice that skill or disposition until the success is internalized and validated by the badge process. Furthermore, we put expiration dates on the badges, as practice and attitudes often should be updated over time with new practice, research, and techniques that further student learning.

In all, we desire autonomy and freedom for our team at Matchbook within a framework and process that influences the collective good and individual growth. A huge premise in our efforts is that we must continue to be explicit about how our work directly correlates to student learning and adult capacity. We are confident that our current practice will help employees develop a monogamous relationship at Matchbook Learning for many years to come. We seek an end to promiscuous professional development, because it fractures the core understanding between our team and our schools. Most importantly, it inhibits the kind of acceleration we seek for our students and the opportunities that await them downstream.

From Bryan Setser and Amy Swann, "An End to Promiscuous Professional Development," *Matchbook News* (blog), May 20, 2016, www.matchbooklearning.com/news/promiscuous -professional-development.

At Sanborn Regional High School, the Freshman Learning Community emerged as a fully collaborative and energized, powerful learning community of teachers who worked with grade 9 students. Much like the professionals in the

Matchbook Learning model, the teachers went deeply into their learning and the application of what they learned. They were given the resources of control of their time. The positive professional culture across grade 9 was palpable, as was the evidence of the growth mind-set that developed professionally as teachers designed learner pathways to address issues of personalization. The balance began to tip from teacher-centric to student-centric learning models. Soon after, the sophomore teachers formed their own learning community, customizing it to the tenth-grade level of learning and development. At the junior and senior level, students are given the opportunity to explore career academies, early college-credit opportunities, and some ELOs.

Moving from Academics to Personal Success Skills (Work Study Practices)

By the beginning of the 2013–2014 school year, the Sanborn School District had developed its competency framework, furthered the design of rigorous performance tasks and assessments, refined its K–12 grading system, and began to develop personalized learning pathways for students. In short, Sanborn was one of the few districts that had systematized CBE in grades K–12. It was not a fait accompli. To this day, no one in Sanborn will tell you that the journey is finished. The district is currently part of a No Grades, No Grades (NG2) collaborative, working with other schools to break the shackles of grade-cohort learning. Yet as the framework for CBE was shaping up nicely at Sanborn, one dimension of the work needed attention: the personal success skills, or work study practices. At each level in Sanborn, the work study practices were different. Ellen Hume-Howard worked with the teachers and leaders to again gather their identified skills under the banner of the state-adopted work study practices: collaboration, creativity, communication, and self-direction.

When teachers began integrating work study practices into their designs for instruction and assessment, it was a game changer in the classroom. The growth mind-set embraced by the teachers, as well as the results from the students, is described in "Voices from the Field: Work Study Practices (Personal Success Skills)," by Terry Bolduc, an outstanding teacher at Memorial School.

VOICES FROM THE FIELD
WORK STUDY PRACTICES (PERSONAL SUCCESS SKILLS)

By Terry Bolduc, Grade 5 Teacher, Memorial School, Newton, New Hampshire

As our district moves toward a competency-based grading system, it became evident that we needed to separate work study grades from academic ones. If we truly were to see competency in our students, their academic grades could not include a gain or loss of credit depending on whether they turned in their homework or came prepared to class.

With this new understanding, I clearly realized that I would need to help my students understand our expectations for work study practices and how they could improve in this important area of school. I spent time modeling examples of works study practices using literature and then connecting those models to real-world examples in our everyday school life. This simple shift in focus brought a deep level of understanding about work study practices and their importance. Students were more responsible about their work because they knew what the expectations were. They were also more empathetic to each other because they understood what the word meant and how empathy helped us all grow as a community, and they were better equipped to regulate themselves and each other throughout their day.

All this deeper understanding, this metacognition, seeped into the children's academics. My students knew that failing was okay if they used their failure as a reason to try again. They knew they were responsible for their learning and that I was there to help them when they needed me. At the end of the year, students answered some questions about how learning more about CARES, Sanborn's elementary-level work study practice system, helped them in fifth grade. I leave you with a quote from one of my students:

Learning in 5B [the fifth-grade team] has affected me personally by just being a better person for our classroom and at my house and even sports. I have thought I've always been a good student, but this year I really know I really improved. I can really see a difference in school, home, and even at sports. I know this isn't part of the question, but I would want to just say thank you for helping me be a better person in many different ways.

Carrying the Torch into the Future

In May 2014, Sanborn's K–12 group of teacher leaders and administrators met for a day-long facilitated discussion to finalize their grade-reporting system. Because of the collective work in the areas of assessment and grade refinements, they could agree on the same competency-based grading scales across the district, for grades K–12. In the years leading up to this work, the elementary and secondary reporting systems evolved until they could agree on the same grade-reporting criteria in each of the K–12 grades. Sanborn Regional School District continues to evolve toward a more personalized, competency-based system of teaching and learning. It continually seeks out expertise to continue this journey. However, the district is clear that the journey is of its own making. For the past several years, Sanborn has opened its doors to hundreds of visitors. This invitation to view, ask questions, probe, and discuss has only made the work more valuable to the district's own shareholders and its visitors. District and school administrators and teachers have presented at statewide, regional, and national opportunities to share their work with others.

Two years ago, the demand for visits was so great that it was becoming a disruption to the team because it was spending too much time hosting visits. To solve this barrier to the district's progress, the team members created a design studio whose purpose was to have schools and districts send teams during the summer to learn about all aspects of Sanborn's model. The design studio was framed so that keynote addresses and shorter presentations were based on all topics in Sanborn's model. Several times during the day, teams in attendance have time to meet and discuss their experiences and think through how they might take their learning into their own designs for their districts. They could also arrange to have any of the Sanborn team meet with them to provide coaching. Hume-Howard, Sanborn's curriculum coordinator, reflects on her experience of the Sanborn transformation:

> Thinking about the work our district has done over the last several years to become a K–12 competency-based organization, I could easily describe the experience as challenging, transformative, and inspiring. But in reality, for me, the work has gone beyond just the excitement of being part of an initiative to improve education in our district. For me, the experience has been a fulfilment

of realizing the culmination of everything I have believed as an educator, everything that I knew was not working for kids and that needed to change. For me, the transformation has been about shifting students to the center of decisions, rather than adjusting for the benefit of adults. The system needed to prioritize learning, not the management of variables that didn't have a direct impact on student learning. The system needed to recognize our students as a driving force for decisions.

What has been most rewarding along the way is that my impressions of what needed to improve in our own district in education were shared with so many of my colleagues here at Sanborn and more broadly in other districts in the state and in the Department of Education. Collectively, we all knew that everything—from how we scheduled students, selected programs and materials, and created courses to how we assessed student achievement or designed curricula—had to focus on the needs of students.

Today, I look at the transformation of education at Sanborn and I know we have more work to do. But in my heart, I know we have built a system that puts students at the center of learning and provides the incentives for teachers to continue to make education about kids.

WHAT WILL BE *YOUR* STORY?

Neither Chugach nor Sanborn could foretell where they would be today. They simply chose the right direction—student learning. They used that as their compass to shape their work and stepped back from the traditional top-down model of management. They created professional spaces for their staff, much like how the working world in our society creates high-quality products. Think about the possibilities in telling your story.

Recently, as the competency fellow for 2Revolutions, a national education design lab, I was working with Adam Rubin, a 2Revolutions founder; Rachel Lopkin, a program associate; and the leadership team in a very large Virginia school district. The district was hoping to move toward a personalized learning model and to break through with a new statewide accountability program. We spent time thinking through the district's building blocks for its future-of-learning model. The district had already worked on its portrait of a graduate and had focused on project-based learning as its entry point into the work.[6] We began with the 2Revolutions building blocks for personalized, competency-based learning (figure 9.1). Our aim was to begin to concretize the strands of work to develop the district's vision of the graduate. It was an opportunity for the district leadership to understand their portals of entry in developing a comprehensive plan for professional learning for the district.

Rubin began the activity by telling the group of district administrators that there was nothing special about what was at the top of the block pile depicted in the figure. Every building block had importance in whatever order the group would place the blocks, depending on the district's portrait of the graduate.

My role was to use cognitive coaching skills with each group to help the participants discern what they valued, what they felt had greater or less importance in the work, and which current teaching and learning practices in the district were connected to each of the blocks. They essentially opened each block and placed their local work it was connected to in each block. In a virtual world, I envisioned that one could highlight each block, and the groups' local district "connects"

FIGURE 9.1 2Revolutions building blocks for personalized learning

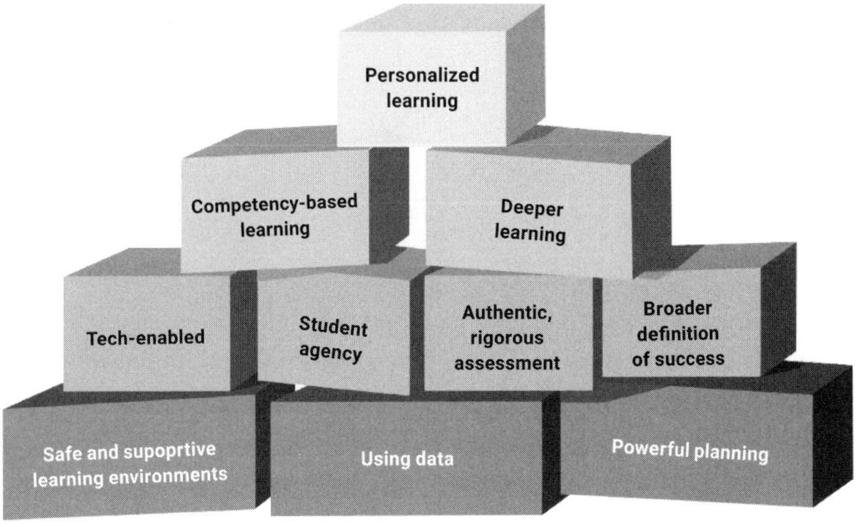

Source: "Building Blocks of Personalization," 2Revolutions, 2016. Reprinted with permission.

would appear as a pop-up. Further enlightening the planning session, each group spoke to what its arrangement of the blocks meant to the group and why the members had arranged the blocks in the configuration they were presenting to the whole group. This exploratory activity helped the district move forward in understanding the various parts of the transformation to CBE. In the end, they placed "deeper learning" as their top block because it best represented the district's recent work in project-based learning and their recognition that their graduation competencies required a personalized learning approach that was competency based.

How would *you* arrange these building blocks? Would CBE be at the top? What about personalized learning? Would move-on-when-ready be at the top? Clearly, your team should agree on how your system of learning will clearly and openly align the goals of your school or district with your vision.

Throughout the years of development in the Sanborn Regional School District and several others in New Hampshire who chose to align their competency work system-wide, the next frontier in CBE was opened. These districts essentially proved that they were ready to become one of the first districts in the United States to pilot a new accountability program based on the principles of CBE. That accountability program is the subject of the next chapter.

Chapter 10

New Hampshire Performance Assessment for Competency Education (NH PACE)

THE ARCHITECTURE FOR COMPETENCY EDUCATION in New Hampshire wouldn't be complete without pushing the envelope of traditional teaching, learning, assessment, *and* accountability. The NCLB era put a focus on the results of statewide testing that was mandated at specific grade levels and within a specified time frame. This stronger accountability for student outcomes ushered in with NCLB in 2002 required students to annually test in reading and mathematics in grades 3–8 and once in high school with an approved statewide assessment test. Science was also tested in grades 4, 8, and 10 at the state level. The results of the mathematics and ELA tests were then evaluated and disaggregated to further determine the accountability status of the school or district within the state.

In the years after its introduction, the testing took on a high-stakes nature as sanctions for lack of improvement in Adequate Yearly Progress (AYP) in student outcomes on these tests were exacted on schools. Failure to show improvement over time meant that students could transfer to other schools within a district; tutoring would be offered to students; or, given a long-term lack of improvement in student outcomes, the state could step in to restructure or close schools that failed to improve. Although by 2005, some flexibility to address student achievement was allowed at the state level, NCLB, as it was originally passed, needed reauthorization. From 2007 through 2015, states began requesting waivers under the existing language of NCLB.[1]

During these years, New Hampshire's annual state assessment in reading, mathematics, and science was the New England Common Assessment Program (NECAP), which was administered and used in determining school or district AYP. Also during this time, however, the state was seeing significant development in establishing CBE in both policy and practice.

BUILDING THE FOUNDATION FOR A NEW ACCOUNTABILITY SYSTEM

Competency, by its very nature, requires multiple and varied assessments to demonstrate and evaluate proficiency. In New Hampshire, there was a growing concern that we were building competency-based systems while the assessments required to determine accountability did not align very well to a once-a-year high-stakes test. Because competency requires performance or demonstration of learning, the New Hampshire Department of Education partnered with the Center for Collaborative Education (www.cce.org) to provide statewide professional development to teach school-based teams how to design high-quality performance tasks and their assessments. The training group offered this professional development directly in the schools, helping staff become more adept at competency alignment, high-quality task design using DOK, and rubric design. Protocols to validate and calibrate tasks and rubric design guided the teacher development work.

During 2012–2013, the performance assessment work was gaining traction throughout the state. While several pioneering districts in systemic K–12 CBE were moving their work forward, several key partners began conversations. As the state's Department of Education competency education consultant, I have worked wherever there is a need for district outreach and in support of projects within the state. Monthly meetings at the department with Center for Collaborative Education partners guided the performance assessment planning. Joining the meetings was Scott Marion of the Center for Assessment. Marion worked closely with the department in many areas, including accountability. Joe DiMartino of the Center for Secondary School Redesign also participated in the monthly meetings because his federal Investing in Education grant-funded work was closely tied to performance assessment in several New Hampshire high schools participating in the grant work over several years.

At one point in the spring of 2013, the climate seemed right to think about competency-based performance assessment as a new approach to accountability. Over several months, we looked to our pioneering districts to possibly pilot a new approach to accountability.

READY TO GO

Paul Leather, New Hampshire's deputy commissioner of education, has been a passionate advocate at all levels of CBE and with most of the stakeholders in competency education nationally. In 2011, New Hampshire was invited into the Innovation Lab Network of the Council for Chief State School Officers. As a member of this innovation network, we participated in conference calls and meetings to further develop innovative CBE practices that supported personalized learning for our students. By the spring of 2013, in our monthly meetings at the department, we decided that we were ready to file for a request to the US Department of Education (USDE) to pilot a new accountability plan for our state, and PACE was born. The state Department of Education began the long process of applying to USDE. By late spring or early summer, four districts came forward to participate in this opportunity. Each district had its own distinct profile of, and level of development for, its CBE system:

▸ *Epping School District:* a small district having one elementary, one middle, and one high school. Epping had developed its competencies for grades 6–12, was a participant in the training sessions in performance assessment, and had developed its grading philosophy statement and grading system for grades 6–12.

▸ *Sanborn Regional School District:* a medium-sized district having two elementary schools, one middle school, and one high school. Sanborn had K–12 competencies and competency-based grading systems in place. It had also participated in the performance assessment training.

▶ *Rochester School District:* a large urban district with eight elementary schools, one large middle school, and one large high school. The district also has a career technical high school and an alternative high school. Rochester had developed its K–12 competency-based grading system according to performance indicators defined in each of their content areas. The district had developed a sophisticated assessment and grading philosophy for grades K–12. It had participated in the performance assessment cohort, but the work was just gaining some attention in the district.

▶ *Souhegan High School:* a district unto itself in Amherst. It serves a regional district of schools (students from surrounding towns attend Souhegan because those smaller towns do not have their own high schools) but is governed by its own board. Souhegan opened its doors in 1992 as a member of the Coalition of Essential Schools and continues to operate using the tenets of that model. The school came to PACE with a highly developed performance assessment system. Although it was using traditional grading, its use of defined learner expectations in its grading was remarkable.

In the fall of 2013, the New Hampshire delegation attended the Innovation Lab Network meeting in Kentucky. Members of the delegation included representatives of the PACE districts and the project partners. Our New Hampshire group received feedback from Linda Darling-Hammond and other attendees on its proposed application for PACE. We were feverishly trying to solve the evolving sets of issues in designing a comprehensive accountability system based on the core beliefs of CBE. We were trying to develop a new accountability system that would pilot the use of performance assessments in place of high-stakes, primarily multiple-choice tests, while still allowing for some standardized testing that could compare outcomes with other states for the purposes of federal accountability.

At that point in time, we were moving toward replacing our state assessment test, NECAP, to the Smarter Balanced Assessment Consortium (SBAC). After hours of work in October 2013, we felt comfortable that we had developed a grade 3 through high school system of balanced assessments with a schedule of performance assessments at each grade level. The pilot assessment system that was devised is made of three components:

▶ The SBAC test in reading and mathematics, administered once in every grade *span*: grades 3–5, grades 6–8, and grade 11 (currently the SAT has replaced the grade 11 SBAC test).

▶ Scores from performance assessments in reading and mathematics in years that the SBAC is not given; the NECAP science assessment in grades 4, 8, and high school would be replaced by performance-based assessment.

▶ Grades derived from competency-based grading throughout the year and recorded in the district's student information system.

Although the total plan would call for more than one teacher-developed performance assessment across each grade level, the plan for the pilot year, 2013–2014, if granted, was to create a collaborative of teachers across the districts to design performance tasks and their assessment criteria and to administer the tasks that spring, embedded within the units of instruction. Ellen Hume-Howard of Sanborn led the ELA task development; Mary Moriarty, assistant superintendent of Rochester, led the mathematics task development; and I took on the leadership of the science task development. This teacher collaborative provided a measure of consistency in the development of the work products across content areas and grade levels.

LAUNCH!

The New Hampshire Department of Education did receive the go-ahead from USDE to develop PACE in the fall of 2013–2014, but did not receive the actual approval of the pilot until March 2014. During that interim period, there were monthly conferences with the USDE to continually clarify and question our work. As the months passed, we were confronted with challenges in process and product. To smooth out some of the operational challenges, the superintendents of each district met each month to chart the course for logistics and work load for each content strand. District leadership also needed to communicate with one another on how the work was progressing at the teacher level and to try to solve problems that emerged. For example, for some performance tasks, the implementation window of time was set for the same window of time as SBAC testing, which stretched technology resources and usage within their buildings.

Since performance tasks were embedded within the regular units of instruction, we had to clarify the difference between scaffolding during learning and conducting a summative assessment of students. One of the biggest challenges was grappling with scoring. The scoring rubric was developed by the teachers specifically for the performance task. Most of the tasks, by being embedded within a unit of work, extended over a period. For some tasks, the work needed to be entered into the local grade book and recorded as local assessments, yet the scoring rubric scales for PACE did not line up exactly with the district's scales in its local grading system. These and several more unanticipated issues seemed to pop up as we were doing this work.

One area that required quite a bit of discernment and problem solving was the comparability and exactness of the tasks being developed. Traditional state assessment tests are basically given in the same short window of testing time and with essentially the same test administered to each cohort of students. This consistency is the best-case scenario for the comparability of data across schools and districts. And because the same test is given with items that have been proven valid and reliable, it is much easier to compare cohorts of students taking those tests within the same school, district, or state.

Performance assessment challenged that notion. We weren't sure how far from that perfect model our new PACE assessments would stray from the exactness and comparability measures necessary for an accountability system. For example, in ELA, students in the same grade level across three school districts may have read different texts before responding to the same prompt. Was the task the same? No, they read different source material. Then, how can you guarantee that their scores are comparable? A machine will score a student test in the same way each time. However, what happens to the reliability of test scores when different teachers score student work? Part of the requirements of PACE was a multistage peer review process and support to ensure that appropriate rigor was comparable within and among schools and districts. There needed to be an alignment of the proposed system of assessment with competencies and a plan for aggregating and reporting annual achievement and growth results.

For performance tasks to be part of a system of assessments as students grow in their college and career readiness, the work study practices also needed assessment.

For each PACE task, local districts may also include their work study practices as part of their local assessment scoring.

We had to do some heavy lifting in supporting teachers across the districts to ensure quality and comparability of assessment results. This was especially true in the Rochester district, where because of large cohorts of grade-level teachers across eight schools, it was difficult to provide the access and time for teachers to collaborate. A monthly schedule of PLC meetings built into the school year in the larger schools and across the smaller schools provided embedded personal development to support task design, validation, and calibration.

The first year of PACE ended with a round of summer work. Samples of student work were collected for teachers to then blind-score them to test the reliability of the scores. The Center for Assessment provided the guidelines for this work. Further work in standard setting brought teachers together to examine the same assessment given by different teachers in different districts because of the need to examine comparability.

In this first year of PACE task design, many of these issues were raised. The result was a stronger program. The goal of each subsequent year of the program was to increase the bank of PACE tasks so that more than one performance task would be given each year. Performance tasks have also been used in the other disciplines. New Hampshire developed its arts competencies in 2014, and since that time, arts teachers across the state have begun creating performance assessments using these new competencies.

LEARNING BY DOING

All this work informed the development of PACE in the second year. By 2015, more districts had expressed an interest in becoming PACE districts. However, not all districts came to the table with the same readiness exhibited by the original four districts. For that reason, a tier system was developed to provide the right measure of support for interested districts. My role in year two of the program shifted from working with the implementing districts, deemed tier 1, to working with tier 2 and tier 3 districts. For 2015–2016, Epping, Sanborn Regional, Rochester, Souhegan, Concord, and Monroe School Districts, as well as Seacoast Charter School, were all implementing PACE. The Seacoast Charter School and

Monroe district had participated as planning districts in the first year of PACE, while Concord's level of readiness made it a great candidate for implementation.

For tiers 2 and 3 schools, we needed to determine what types of support they would need to continue their forward journey toward becoming an implementing district. I conducted on-site interviews with district leadership across the full spectrum of their curriculum and competencies analysis, their assessment strategies, their instructional assets, the status of their PLC development, their grading systems, and their technology resources. From there, Mariane Gfroerer, our PACE project manager, worked with these local districts to bring them along in their development by targeting project resources to their needs.

A district is deemed a tier 2 district if it has been involved in performance assessment training and needs continuing support and planning to be ready to implement the performance tasks as part of their district's accountability. They would also be ready to use local grading and administer SBAC by grade span. This support may be needed in their competency development work, grading system, or PLC development. A tier 3 district is one that needs performance assessment training in addition to district development around competencies and grading. Once districts are deemed tier 2, regular meetings are held for districts to plan and collaborate.

One strategy that worked well in the first year of PACE was to blur district lines when delivering professional development. To be clear, the success of PACE lies with the engagement of teachers in developing the tasks, validating and calibrating them, administering them, and then scoring and further participating in the reliability and comparability work. New Hampshire, although smaller than many other states, needed to develop ways to scale this work from several districts that were ready to a statewide model. Having teachers collaborate across districts not only increased efficiency but also brought rich thinking to the work. The cross-pollination of ideas and experiences enhanced the development of this work.

More districts are coming forward to become PACE districts as the system is developing. The New Hampshire Department of Education has now formalized a readiness matrix or tool for districts to use in their decision to become a PACE district.[2] Yet, the department does not require that districts participate. They can continue to choose the SBAC as their accountability system. Tier 2 and 3 districts continue with this consortium until they are ready to implement PACE. This also speaks to the local control found in the "Live Free or Die" state. On a positive note, when a district brings before its local school board a request to become a PACE district, the proposed transition seems to address the distrust and objections that have previously burdened state-mandated testing. The first year of PACE coincided with the first year of SBAC, where the opt-out clause for the consortium was in play. In considering their districts' requests to become PACE districts, school boards have generally looked favorably on the potential decrease in the frequency of SBAC testing and the greater role of teachers in determining student proficiency across multiple measures over a longer period.

The performance tasks that were developed during that first year have undergone review and improvement by the work teachers conducted during the summer of 2015 and in sessions that followed. The time spent reviewing student work was most advantageous in improving the quality of the tasks and rubrics. In 2015–2016, teachers administered the same tasks as those in 2014–2015 while developing another set of performance tasks to add to the bank of tasks. There is a cyclic nature to the work: continual task development, improvement, and implementation.

In believing that performance assessment results are comparable to SBAC, we also needed to provide metrics to that effect in accountability data from PACE districts. The New Hampshire Department of Education released the 2014–2015 PACE accountability results in December 2015 (http://education.nh.gov /assessment-systems/pace.htm), demonstrating that individual proficiency could be determined using the metrics of SBAC, performance task scores, and competency-based grading.

THE FUTURE OF NEW ACCOUNTABILITY SYSTEMS

While all eyes were on New Hampshire in developing PACE as a possible national model for a state-based accountability system, the national Elementary and Secondary Education Act was being reauthorized. New Hampshire Deputy Commissioner Paul Leather testified before the US Senate Education Committee during hearings that led to the final passage of the Every Student Succeeds Act (ESSA) that was signed into law by President Obama on December 10, 2015. Since then, as the rule-making process for the law has taken place, educators have a clearer sense of the parameters that states now have in setting their accountability systems. The act is an extensive law that will require further study for policy makers at the state level as well as local education agencies.[3]

In this new ESSA era, states can take advantage of the law that allows them to define coherent systems of assessments for accountability purposes. New accountability programs will provide better measures of student readiness for college and career while also providing assessment data to enable teachers to best respond to their students' learning.

LEARNING FROM THE PAST TO BUILD THE ROBUST MODELS OF THE FUTURE

As new personalized CBE models emerge, we must continue to examine the research data that emerges. Locally, schools that have shifted to CBE may have microscale data on which to grow into the future. Trying to yield multiple measures across many models will be challenging. Leaders must understand that academics alone are not the only measures to determine success along the way, yet we can begin there and build on that foundation. The emerging data from research shows that we are headed in the right direction. The Rand Corporation studied sixty-two schools using CBE approaches for two years. The results showed (1) positive effects on learning outcomes in reading and mathematics; (2) greater growth by students with lower starting achievement, demonstrating greater growth rates than their peers; and (3) widespread, statistically positive results. These results, in addition to other data in the study, suggest promising effects of personalized learning on student achievement.[4] In creating a system of equity for many of our children, we should let go of many of the one-size-fits-all methods and bravely try new approaches that will mean greater success for these students. These successes translate into a much brighter future for them when they leave us. Consider "Voices from the Field: Vincent Thur," which describes the experiences of Vincent Thur, who has been working with overaged, undercredited youth in Chicago.

VOICES FROM THE FIELD

CBE FOR STUDENTS FACING CHALLENGING SITUATIONS

By Vincent Thur, Youth Connections Charter School, Chicago

Chicago has a charter of nineteen alternative high schools that are making the transition from an educational system relying on a time-based Carnegie unit to a CBE model. The charter's philosophy is rooted in the belief that highly effective schools can produce change in student's lives by diminishing the effects of a student's past negative experiences and providing the foundation to help break the cycle of poverty that they are mired in. Personalizing learning in a way that meets the challenges of serving urban youth and their accompanying dispositions (frequent and voluntary habits of thinking and doing) is daunting.

The urban youth in these high schools are disconnected in that they have been out of school or are off-track for a high school credential, and the traditional system has failed them multiple times. The average student is eighteen and has only ten credits out of the eighteen necessary to graduate, and many students are at risk of aging out before they achieve their goal. Their frame of reference and dispositions are shaped by social-emotional factors (e.g., exposure to trauma); a recent study found that over 60 percent of students had experienced some form of violence.[5] In addition, over 80 percent of the students face the academic challenge of reading below the 25th percentile.

In 2011, the charter's stakeholders listed four competencies that are necessary for students to be successful in their future academic and professional lives. These competencies underpin the entire curricular framework: critical thinking, effective communication, creative exploration, and active contributor. The charter's curricular framework is built around teaching and assessing these four skills while providing students a personalized learning environment based on transformational organizing principles that include putting students in disorienting experiences (i.e., situations that they've never experienced before) and focusing on building resiliency and academic self-efficacy through autonomous learning. Now that the framework is developed, the charter will begin to administer an academic educational plan to assess where students are emotionally and academically when they enroll. Students will then work with staff to establish a personalized postsecondary pathway based on several pertinent aspects of their academic and personal life. In addition to a transcript analysis, a barrier survey will help determine the impact of barriers to their education. The staff will also uncover previous support that was helpful to the students and any recommended interventions. Additionally, the staff will prepare an intervention plan to address the barriers and will conduct frequent analysis of the students' responses to these interventions.

From there, some campuses enroll their students in traditional classes. The goal of instruction is to begin at the student's present functioning level and to strive to personalize learning by engaging students in a growth-model approach that uses assessment to measure a student's acquisition of skills. Schools utilize a thematic, interdisciplinary approach to instruction built around personalized long-term investigative projects that focus on the crucial knowledge in each discipline. These projects require a student to demonstrate understanding by applying his or her knowledge and skills to identify and solve complex, real-world problems. All exhibitions of learning must include aspects from each of the four cross-cutting competencies, provide the student with multiple ways to choose a topic and present his or her learning, and use exhibition rubrics to formatively assess learning before a student can complete the summative exhibition of learning. Student mastery is captured on student check-off lists that incorporate "I can" statements to measure mastery around each cross-cutting competency and provide students with real-time feedback on their mastery. Students are at the heart of the learning process, and teachers act as facilitators who present content from whole to part, with emphasis on big ideas and questions, and who design individual stand-alone modules that revolve around experiential learning, inquiry, and exploration of the world and careers around the students.

Other campuses begin by enrolling all the new students in reengagement programs, which last about ten weeks, and seek to reengage students and build their resiliency, academic self-efficacy, and autonomous learning by exposing students to disorienting experiences. The reengagement approach is meant to provide a bridge between the social-emotional needs of the student and the academic requirements of the classroom. These schools realize that once they have identified student barriers, to reach these disconnected youth, they need to first provide essential services or refer the students to organizations that can provide support that the campus cannot. One approach is to use the four cross-cutting competencies and student voice and choice in topics to bridge the students' social-emotional needs with their academic ones. Once the students have demonstrated competency in the social-emotional indicators and cross-cutting competencies and begun to demonstrate increased resiliency through the different disorientating experiences, they are enrolled in the rest of the school curriculum that is also built around the competencies.

The challenge of reengaging disconnected youth faced with a myriad of barriers and providing the necessary academic and social-emotional bridges to connect to career and college is real, but with our schools' competency- and mastery-based approaches, students can move at their own pace and receive all the support they need, when they need it.

Now, more than ever before, we have the opportunity to define education in ways that are the most customized and personalized to our learners. For many, the realization that we can no longer just fix the problems of today's education with yesterday's remedies is hard medicine to swallow. It may be easier to think that we can try just one more thing that we haven't thought of earlier to come up with that fix. Yet the reality is that fixing the old system has not worked well for a long time, and we have much to do to catch up with thinking differently about a new architecture for our schools. Many school models, both public and private, have bravely taken on a vision for their futures—a vision that is robust and timely. Consider the experience of Danny Medved, principal of the Denver School of Innovation and Sustainable Design, in "Voices from the Field: Denver School of Innovation and Sustainable Design."

VOICES FROM THE FIELD
DENVER SCHOOL OF INNOVATION AND SUSTAINABLE DESIGN

By Danny Medved, principal of Denver School of Innovation and Sustainable Design

Denver School of Innovation and Sustainable Design (DSISD) is a competency-based high school in Denver Public Schools. DSISD's vision drives all elements of the school's design and programming: "To empower all students to own their learning, shape their dreams, and create a better world." Our founding team was made up of a passionate group of highly competent, committed teachers and leaders who wanted to re-shape the way education is delivered by reshaping the school as the greatest vehicle for change. The team hailed from eclectic backgrounds that ranged from founders of small high schools to people with expeditionary learning backgrounds, and experience that ranged from blended learning pedagogy to alternative pathways to teaching.

In addition to a committed founding team, DSISD borrows several best practices from effective high school designs, such as galvanizing the school around a shared vision of personalized learning, emphasizing positive youth development, distributing leadership across staff, and employing intentional practices for data-driven instruction and project-based learning. However, the school is most remarkable in its commitment to bringing CBE theory to life in practical and scalable ways at the school level.

To ensure that the school's design and ongoing operation is connected to CBE theory, our team uses the International Association for K–12 Online Learning (iNACOL) five-part working definition of CBE as a plumb line:

- Students advance upon demonstrated mastery.
- Competencies include explicit, measurable, transferable learning objectives that empower students.
- Assessment is meaningful and a positive learning experience for students.
- Students receive rapid, differentiated support based on their individual learning needs.
- Learning outcomes emphasize competencies that include application and creation of knowledge, along with the development of important skills and dispositions.[6]

CBE models differ sharply from the traditional model of seat time and Carnegie units, which use the passage of time and the awarding of grades to determine a student's readiness for the next grade or stage of education, such as the transition from high school to college. In contrast, CBE allows students to move on to the next grade or skill, depending on their demonstrations of mastery of specific competencies, which are anchored in rigorous standards. Likewise, this approach more readily allots targeted support and interventions to students who have not yet demonstrated a required skill. This support can include extended time to demonstrate mastery, additional teacher- or peer-provided support, or alternative means for students to show mastery. In addition to measuring academic standards, competencies may also measure noncognitive abilities, such as social-emotional competencies.

Though CBE is intuitive in its student-centered approach to measuring mastery, it does require a nontraditional and intentionally designed infrastructure to be effectively implemented and monitored. More simply put, our DSISD founding team knew that unless we developed school-based systems for each element of the definition, we would revert to the traditional paradigms that have governed education for the last century. Therefore, we set out to identify how each of the elements of the iNACOL definition comes to life at DSISD.

While there is a bigger and ever-adapting story to tell about how each of the essential five parts in iNACOL's definition come to life at our school, the second element ("Competencies include explicit, measurable, transferable learning objectives that empower students") and the fifth ("Learning outcomes emphasize competencies that include application and creation of knowledge, along with the development of important skills and dispositions") played a critical role in helping the school identify its unique vision anchored identity. DSISD's qualities of innovators include personal academic excellence, lifelong learning and citizenship, innovative thinking and action, and transformative leadership.

Essential Domains of Learning: The Qualities of an Innovator

The school's vision is operationalized through the building blocks of the four qualities of an innovator and the innovator competencies that undergird each of them:

- *Strong academics*: develop a mastery of academic standards.
- *Lifelong learning and citizenship*: know and invest in yourself and your community.
- *Innovative thinking and action*: apply academic knowledge in creative and solution-oriented ways.
- *Transformative leadership*: boldly lead to address the challenges of today as a values-driven professional and citizen.

These four domains of learning that our team felt were necessary are areas of skills for a student who would be ready to lead and innovate in the twenty-first century. Strong academics, while critically important and intentionally planned for in DSISD's design, only make up one-fourth of the equation. The design team considered soft skills equally important, if not more so, for successful adult life in today's fast-paced world.

Getting More Explicit: Creating the Innovator Competencies and Portfolio System

The four innovator qualities provided the framework to make our school's vision a reality for each student. Our team also needed to go one layer deeper by making our competencies and experiences more explicit, as the iNACOL definition suggests. This next layer of work resulted in the development of our innovator competencies. To gain promotion and show mastery at DSISD, students develop a digital portfolio and obtain badges for each competency. Though the more traditional, academic-focused competencies are heavily anchored in student mastery of standards, such as Next Generation Science and Common Core ELA and math, students gain mastery of the soft-skill competencies by gathering artifacts, personally reflecting on their own progress, and applying competencies such as the ability to creatively express themselves, design with empathy, and invest in others. An artifact is simply evidence. It goes beyond a test score, although that is evidence also. An artifact may be what the student deems important, such as a digital portfolio, podcast, or video. Because these reflections on growth and mastery are highly personal to each student, evidence of mastery may vary as well. Finally, students can celebrate their progress as they earn badges and credentials in these areas. These credentials can be distributed publicly as well as through social media like Facebook and LinkedIn. Students can even produce high-quality college application material from the credentials they have stored in the Locker and Space application through the Coalition for Access, Affordability, and Success.

To structure student learning to support growth in soft-skill competencies, the team designed DSISD in a way to ensure that students would have experiences that build the desired innovator competencies.* Though our portfolio system and the learning experiences that students engage in are a work in progress, our team has a plan

---

*The school's student competencies are described and elaborated at Denver School of Innovation and Sustainable Design, "Our Approach: Competencies," Denver Public Schools, 2014, http://dsisd .dpsk12.org/our-approach/competencies.

that we believe will scale with our founding class. If we keep working the plan and reflecting along the way, the theory guiding our design will turn into a lived reality. A day in the life of a typical DSISD student is the result of many elements coming together to change how school is done: the provision of a blank canvas for new school design; the convergence of an incredible team of educators; the definition of, and research on, the best practices to anchor the work in; the creation of a shared vision; and the design of competencies and learning experiences that can bring that vision to life.

The two "Voices from the Field" at the end of this chapter highlight how we must approach our designs for meaningful learning for our students. Each story has a different beginning, different profiles of students, and a different developmental arc to its work. However, the schools' priorities were like-minded. With that laser focus on student success in preparing their students for life after high school, the schools designed wraparound systems of learning that addressed both academics and personal success skills in vibrant school communities built with intentionality. We can't lose a generation of students simply because we lack the courage and the fortitude to dig in and do this work now. It does seem daunting, but we can continue to innovate in assessing students according to their ability to transfer their acquired content and skills, and we can measure student growth in their personal success skills leading to graduation.

What will the architecture of CBE look like ten, fifteen, or twenty years from now? If we do this right, it will have evolved and grown to be more responsive to society's need for an educated workforce. Our educators will probably be working to support their own learning and their students' learning using a toolkit of resources that today is just emerging. Technology will be a part of our industry in the same way it is in other industries, as it provides greater equity and access to the learning resources our students need.

As this new architecture evolves, we will come to actualize structures that acknowledge that we as learners grow not just in the learning that takes place in brick-and-mortar classrooms but also in the experiences we have in our communities beyond the school day or the defined school year.

Will *you* be the architect of the future of education? If you will be writing your story in five, eight, or ten years, what will you have to say? Your story will be born out of your own creativity as an educator and a leader to move your school or district into the future. Join the many school leaders and teachers who firmly believe that personalized, competency-based education is our future, unshackled by the past.

Glossary

blended learning: Curriculum delivery that uses a combination of face-to-face teaching and learning in a brick-and-mortar school with online curriculum delivery. Blended learning can be customized and adapted to student learning needs.

cognitive-rigor matrix: Content-area matrices developed by Karin Hess that cross-walk Webb's depth of knowledge and Bloom's taxonomy. These matrices are used in designing performance indicators and learning and assessment targets.

college and career readiness: Evidence of competence in academic and personal success skills to enter higher education or the workforce. The graduate has demonstrated the knowledge and skills to independently apply their learning in new situations.

competency-based (dynamic) grading: A comprehensive system of grading that supports a proficiency-based learning and assessment system.

competency validation rubric: The collaborative review of a competency statement through the use of a rubric to determine the statement's strength.

depth of knowledge (DOK): The four levels of depth or complexity of learning; defined by Norman Webb.

differentiation: The use of flexible grouping within whole-class instruction to meet the individual needs of students. Process, content, product, and learning environment are considered when planning differentiated learning opportunities.

district competency: A content-area competency statement used by a district to identify a major concept area of learning on which grade level, grade span, course curriculum, assessment, and grading are anchored.

formative learning and assessment: The knowledge and skills a student must learn to successfully perform tasks. Formative assessment is the feedback given to students while they are learning this defined content and doing the identified skills. Formative assessment data should trigger relearning opportunities, when appropriate, before students move on to summative assessments.

grade-level, grade-span, or course competency: Competency statements customized to the content of a particular grade level, grade span, or course. These competencies represent the major concept areas within a discipline. A competency statement may be derived and customized from a particular district competency statement.

grading philosophy statement: A comprehensive, district-wide set of beliefs and practices that promote fair and responsible competency-based grading by all teachers. The statement defines the purpose of grading and the performance criteria for grading academic and personal success skills within a school district. The research-based, collaboratively designed statement guides all teacher grading practices in communicating student learning within a school district.

graduation competencies: The set of competencies that may include academic and personal success skills required for graduation. Products or demonstrations of learning required for graduation may also be stipulated here.

learning progression: A defined order of learning steps based on content, skills, cognitive reasoning, and complexity that guides the teaching and learning of major concepts within content areas.

performance indicator: An "I can" statement that is both a learning and an assessment target within a unit of work or a performance task. Performance indicators are assessed by students and teachers and should be categorized by depth of knowledge.

performance task: A complex task that is designed within a unit of work and that creates a relevant and rigorous opportunity for students to demonstrate their proficiency in one or more competencies. Performance tasks should promote student choice, voice, and agency.

personal learning plan: A comprehensive journal of learning experiences and goal setting developed by a learner over the course of his or her learning career. It is meant to engage the learner in self-reflection of academic goals, personal success skills, interests, assets, and learning experiences that includes classroom learning, community-based learning, and online and blended learning experiences.

personal success skills (in New Hampshire, called work study practices): Sometimes referred to as dispositions or twenty-first-century skills, this set of skills grows developmentally with the student through the child's learning experiences. These skills should be intentionally designed and assessed by the student and teacher as part of performance tasks.

personalization: The learning design that promotes student-centered and student-directed activities. These learning designs incorporate student choice, voice, and agency in student demonstrations of competency.

standard: Content or skills that define a content area. Clusters of standards are used to create tasks in which students demonstrate a defined level of proficiency.

standards-based grading: A grading system based on best practices in grading as defined by the work of Guskey, Marzano, O'Connor, Wormeli, and other research in standards-based grading practices. The reference criteria in this type of grading are content-area standards only.

summative assessment: The evaluation of the application or transfer of content and skills. Summative assessment is evaluated in performance tasks when students have shown they have acquired the necessary content and skills as part of their formative learning and assessment. These assessments are aligned to competencies and grading criteria.

Notes

PREFACE

1. I use the terms *competency education* and *competency-based education* (CBE) interchangeably in this book. Although this framework is most often called *competency-based education*, it is usually referred to as *competency education* in my home state of New Hampshire.
2. Fred J. Bramante and Rose L. Colby, *Off the Clock: Moving Education from Time to Competency* (Thousand Oaks, CA: Corwin Press, 2012).
3. As explained in the preface, the terms *competency-based education* (CBE) and *competency education* are used interchangeably in this book. As of this writing, this system of education is called *competency education* in the State of New Hampshire, but is more commonly called *CBE* elsewhere in the United States.

CHAPTER 1

1. Chris Sturgis, "Is Competency Education a Disruptive Innovation? The Answer Is No," *CompetencyWorks*, May 8, 2015, www.competencyworks.org/?s=disruptive+innovation&x=0&y=0.
2. Ibid.
3. John D. Bransford, Ann L. Brown, and Rodney R. Cocking, *How People Learn: Brain, Mind, Experience, and School: Expanded Edition* (Washington, DC: National Academy Press, 2000).
4. Joseph E. Zins, Roger P. Weissberg, Margaret C. Wang, and Herbert J. Walberg, *Building Academic Success on Social and Emotional Learning: What Does the Research Say?* (New York: Teachers College Press, 2004).
5. In a CBE system, particularly the one advocated by this book, competency is defined by a level of performance on a task, calibrated to a higher-order level of thinking (level 3 on Web's Depth of Knowledge), the kind of deeper learning required for college and career readiness. Both the task and the rubrics that set out the criteria for competence are given to students in advance and guide the subsequent learning.
6. Chris Sturgis, "Reaching the Tipping Point: Insights on Advancing Competency Education in New England," *CompetencyWorks*, December 27, 2016, www.competencyworks.org/resources/reaching-the-tipping-point-insights-on-advancing-competency-education-in-new-england/#more-14859.

CHAPTER 2

1. Richard Fry, "Millennials Overtake Baby Boomers as American's Largest Generation," *FactTank* (Pew Research Center blog), April 25, 2016, www.pewresearch.org/fact-tank/2016/04/25 /millennials-overtake-baby-boomers.
2. Taposh Bari et al., "Millennial Moms," *Goldman Sachs Equity Research*, May 11, 2015, https:// yhseconomics.wikispaces.com/file/view/Millennial+Parents+GS.pdf.
3. Ibid.
4. Neil Howe, "Introducing the Homeland Generation (Part 1 of 2)," *Forbes*, October 27, 2014, http://onforb.es/10vlOs4.
5. Nathaniel Kendall-Taylor, "Orchestrating Systems and Remodeling Reform: Reframing Education Reform with Simplifying Models," FrameWorks Institute, November 2009, www.frameworks institute.org/assets/files/PDF_Education/orchestrating_systems_and_remodeling_reform.pdf.
6. Susan Bales, "Framing Education Reform: A Frameworks Message Memo," FrameWorks Institute, January 2010, www.frameworksinstitute.org/assets/files/PDF_Education/education _message_memo.pdf

CHAPTER 3

1. H. Lynn Erickson, *Concept-Based Curriculum and Instruction for the Thinking Classroom* (Thousand Oaks, CA: Corwin Press, 2006).
2. National Governors Association, and Chief Council of State School Officers, Common Core State Standards Initiative, "Preparing America's Students for Success," 2010, www.corestandards .org. See also Common Core State Standards Initiative, "Grade 5: Number & Operations in Base Ten; Understand the Place Value System," accessed March 16, 2016, www.corestandards.org /Math/Content/5/NBT/A/1.
3. New Hampshire Department of Education, "New Hampshire College and Career Ready K–8 Mathematics Model Competencies," 2016, http://education.nh.gov/innovations/hs_redesign /documents/english-K-8-2016.pdf.
4. Judith A. Arter and Jay McTighe, *Scoring Rubrics in the Classroom: Using Performance Criteria for Assessing and Improving Student Performance*, Experts in Assessment Series (Thousand Oaks, CA: Corwin Press, 2000).
5. New Hampshire Department of Education, "New Hampshire Common Core State Standards: Aligned English Language Arts and Literacy Competencies," 2013, http://education.nh.gov /innovations/hs_redesign/documents/ccrs-competencies-ela.pdf.
6. Achieve, "The Role of Learning Progressions in Competency-Based Pathways," July 27, 2015, www.achieve.org/learningprogressionsinCBP.
7. Karin Hess, "Developing and Using Learning Progressions as a Schema for Measuring Progress," National Center for the Improvement of Educational Assessment, 2008, www.nciea.org /publications/CCSSO2_KH08.pdf.
8. For K–12 competencies, see New Hampshire Department of Education, "College and Career Ready K–8 English Language Arts Model Competencies." For high school competencies, see New Hampshire Department of Education, "Common Core State Standards: Aligned English Language Arts."
9. Grant Wiggins and Jay McTighe, *The Understanding by Design Guide to Creating High-Quality Units* (Alexandria, VA: Association for Supervision & Curriculum Development, 2011).
10. Epping School District, "Epping High School Biology Syllabus," Epping School District, Epping, New Hampshire, updated July 2015, www.sau14.org/Biology%20syllabus-%20July%202015.pdf.

CHAPTER 4

1. David T. Conley, "A Complete Definition of College and Career Readiness," Educational Policy Improvement Center, May 2, 2012, www.epiconline.org/ccr-definition.

2. Karin Hess and Brian Gong, "Ready for College and Career? Achieving the Common Core Standards and Beyond Through Deeper, Student-Centered Learning," National Center for the Improvement of Educational Assessment, March 2014, www.nmefoundation.org/get attachment/Resources/SCL-2/Ready-for-College-and-Career/Ready-for-College-and-Career .pdf?ext=.pdf.

3. S. Lench, E. Fukuda, and R. Anderson, *Essential Skills and Dispositions: Developmental Frameworks for Collaboration, Creativity, Communication, and Self-Direction* (Lexington, KY: Center for Innovation in Education at the University of Kentucky, 2015).

CHAPTER 5

1. David T. Conley and Linda Darling-Hammond, "Creating Systems of Assessment for Deeper Learning," 2013, Stanford, CA: Stanford Center for Opportunity Policy in Education, https:// edpolicy.stanford.edu/sites/default/files/publications/creating-systems-assessment-deeper -learning_0.pdf

2. Norman L. Webb, "Depth-of-Knowledge Levels for Four Content Areas," March 28, 2002, http://ossucurr.pbworks.com/w/file/fetch/49691156/Norm web dok by subject.

3. Karin Hess, "Cognitive Rigor and Depth of Knowledge," accessed March 16, 2017, www.karin -hess.com/cognitive-rigor-and-dok.

4. Karin Hess, "Cognitive Complexity: Applying Webb DOK to Bloom's Taxonomy," 2006, http:// www.nciea.org/publications/DOK_ApplyingWebb_KH08.pdf.

5. Soung Bae and Kari Kokka, "Engagement Toolkit for Performance Task Writers, Reviewers, and Evaluators, Stanford Center for Opportunity Policy in Education," July 1, 2016, https://edpolicy .stanford.edu/publications/pubs/1424.

6. State of New Hampshire, Department of Education, "NH K–12 Model Science Competencies," April 24, 2014, www.education.nh.gov/innovations/hs_redesign/documents/ccrs-competencies -science.pdf.

7. Kay Burke, *How to Assess Authentic Learning* (Thousand Oaks, CA: Corwin Press, 2005).

8. Lisa Almeida and Larry Ainsworth, *Engaging Classroom Assessments*, Making Standards Work Series (Englewood, CO: Lead + Learn Press, 2009).

9. Rhode Island Department of Education and the National Center for the Improvement of Educational Assessment, "Calibration Protocol for Scoring Student Work: A Part of the Assessment Toolkit," *Ride*, accessed March 27, 2017, www.ride.ri.gov/Portals/0/Uploads/Documents /Teachers-and-Administrators-Excellent-Educators/Educator-Evaluation/Online-Modules /Calibration_Protocol_for_Scoring_Student_Work.pdf.

10. Alec Patton, "Work That Matters: The Teacher's Guide to Project-Based Learning," Paul Hamlyn Foundation, February 2012, www.innovationunit.org/sites/default/files/Teacher's%20Guide% 20to%20Project-based%20Learning.pdf.

11. Summit Public Schools, "Explore a Day in the Life of a Summit Student," Summit Public Schools, Redwood City, CA, accessed March 27, 2017, http://www.summitps.org/student-day ?day=1).

12. Ivan Zuliani and Steven Ellis, "New Hampshire Extended Learning Opportunities: Final Report of Evaluation Findings," May 2011, www.education.nh.gov/innovations/elo/documents /evaluation.pdf.

13. Mariane Gfroerer, "What Is a Good ELO?," in *The NH Extended Learning Opportunities Teacher Handbook* (Concord: NH Department of Education, 2009), www.education.nh.gov/innovations/elo/documents/ResearchReflectionProductandPresentation.pdf.

14. New Hampshire Department of Education, "Extended Learning Opportunities," 2012, www.education.nh.gov/innovations/elo/index.htm.

15. The rubrics can be downloaded at Lebanon High School, "ELO Rubrics," accessed March 27, 2017, https://sites.google.com/a/sau88.net/lhs_elo/elo-rubrics.

CHAPTER 6

1. Association for Middle Level Education, "This We Believe: Keys to Educating Young Adolescents," 2013, available for purchase at www.amle.org/AboutAMLE/ThisWeBelieve/tabid/121/Default.aspx.

2. Colette Connolly, "The Best Alternative High School Programs in Westchester," *Westchester Magazine* March 6, 2015, www.westchestermagazine.com/Westchester-Magazine/March-2015/The-Best-Alternative-High-School-Programs-In-Westchester.

3. Michael B. Horn and Heather Staker, *Blended: Using Disruptive Innovation to Improve Schools* (San Francisco: Jossey-Bass, 2014).

4. Ibid.

CHAPTER 7

1. Thomas Guskey, *On Your Mark: Challenging the Conventions of Grading and Reporting* (Bloomington, IN: Solution Tree, 2014).

2. Epping School District, "Epping High School Grading and Reporting Student Achievement," Epping School District, Epping, NH, August 7, 2014, www.sau14.org/HS%20Grading%20and%20Reporting_approved%208-7-14(1).pdf.

3. New England Secondary School Consortium, "67 New England Institutions of Higher Education Offer Statements of Support for Proficiency-Based Education," http://newenglandssc.org/resources/collegiate-support.

4. Erika Blauth and Sarah Hadjian, "How Selective Colleges and Universities Evaluate Proficiency-Based High School Transcripts: Insights for Students and Schools," April 2016, www.nebhe.org/info/pdf/policy/Policy_Spotlight_How_Colleges_Evaluate_PB_HS_Transcripts_April_2016.pdf.

CHAPTER 8

1. During the first three years of implementation (2009–2012), scores on the California Academic Performance Index (API) increased by 91 points. English language arts (ELA) proficiency rates for ninth-graders increased from 29 to 41 percent; tenth-graders, from 25 to 37 percent; eleventh-graders, from 21 to 42 percent. (CompetencyWorks, "Research, Evaluation and Results: California," n.d., http://competencyworks.pbworks.com/w/page/67261799/Research%2C%20Evaluation%20and%20Results.

2. Grant P. Wiggins and Jay McTighe, *Schooling by Design: Mission, Action, and Achievement* (Alexandria, VA: ASCD, 2007).

3. Chris Sturgis, "Implementation Insights from Pittsfield School District," CompetencyWorks, March 4, 2014, www.competencyworks.org/uncategorized/implementation-insights-from-pittsfield-school-district/#more-6155.

CHAPTER 9

1. Chris Sturgis, "Chugach School District: A Personalized, Performance-Based System," March 2016, www.inacol.org/wp-content/uploads/2016/03/CW_ChugachSchoolDistrict_APersonalized PerformanceBasedSystem.pdf.

2. Ibid.

3. Lawrence W. Lezotte, "Correlates of Effective Schools: The First and Second Generation," Effective Schools Products, Okemos, MI, 1991, www.effectiveschools.com/images/stories/escorrelates .pdf.

4. Richard F. Elmore, *School Reform from the Inside Out: Policy, Practice, and Performance* (Cambridge, MA: Harvard Education Press, 2004.

5. Catherine Miles Grant et al., *Secondary Lenses on Learning Participant Book: Team Leadership for Mathematics in Middle and High Schools* (Thousand Oaks, CA: Corwin, 2009).

6. "Building Blocks of Personalization," 2Revolutions, 2016.

CHAPTER 10

1. Alyson Klein, "No Child Left Behind: An Overview," *Education Week*, April 10, 2015, www .edweek.org/ew/section/multimedia/no-child-left-behind-overview-definition-summary.html.

2. New Hampshire Department of Education, "NH PACE Readiness Tool," June 2016, www .education.nh.gov/assessment-systems/documents/pace-matrix.pdf.

3. Two excellent resources link the new ESSA legislation to planning and implementing competency education. S. Patrick, M. Worthen, D. Frost, and S. Gentz, "Meeting the Every Student Succeeds Act's Promise: State Policy to Support Personalized Learning," Vienna, VA, International Association for K–12 Online Learning (iNACOL), 2016, is a comprehensive review of ESSA with policy recommendations for states that support personalized CBE in preparation for college and career readiness. See also Knowledge Works, "Four Critical Opportunities for States Under the Every Student Succeeds Act (ESSA)," accessed March 27, 2017, www.knowledgeworks.org/sites /default/files/u1/essa-better-approach-assessment.pdf. Designed by KnowledgeWorks, the Center for Assessment, and the Nellie Mae Education Foundation, this graphic shows the shift in expectations from NCLB to ESSA.

4. John Pane, Elizabeth Steiner, Matthew Baird, and Laura Hamilton, "Continued Progress: Promising Evidence on Personalized Learning," RAND Corporation, 2015, www.rand.org/pubs /research_reports/RR1365.html.

5. David Finkelhor et al., "Children's Exposure to Violence: A Comprehensive National Survey," *Juvenile Justice Bulletin*, October 2009, www.ncjrs.gov/pdffiles1/ojjdp/227744.pdf.

6. Susan Patrick, Kathryn Kennedy, and Allison Powell, "Mean What You Say: Defining and Integrating Personalized, Blended and Competency Education," iNACOL, October 2013, www .inacol.org/wp-content/uploads/2015/02/mean-what-you-say.pdf. There were a few minor differences between the original 2011 definition cited earlier in this book and the 2013 definition presented here.

Acknowledgments

I TAKE THIS OPPORTUNITY to acknowledge the support and assistance of Deputy Commissioner Paul Leather of the New Hampshire Department of Education, as well as the support of Mariane Gfroerer, also of the department. Their continued support of my fieldwork in helping schools and districts understand the implications of competency-based learning and grading have continued to shape my thinking. Chris Sturgis of MetisNet has encouraged me to continue writing for CompetencyWorks and has been invaluable in developing this innovation we call competency-based education (CBE). The 2Revolutions team of Adam Rubin, Todd Kern, Jim Stephens, Ali Brown, and Ami Desai continue to challenge my thinking around the future of education and systems design. I am honored to contribute to their groundbreaking work as their Competency Education Fellow. Bryan Setser of Matchbook Learning continues to inspire my creative thinking.

In 2012, I was fortunate to have the opportunity to meet Sandra Dop, formerly of the Iowa Department of Education, and the late Diane Smith from Oregon. Both were passionate about CBE. That meeting in New Orleans forged a wonderful friendship and what we called our Coast-to-Coast Connection. We have been strong voices on the CompetencyWorks advisory group because of this relationship. We checked each other's thinking, shared practices and policy from each other's state, and, as a result, have learned a great deal. We recently lost Diane Smith, who in her passing has left a great legacy for many educators, including Sandra and me. My special thanks to Sandra for the time she has spent with this manuscript questioning my thinking and providing some much-needed edits.

ments

A number of other educators in New Hampshire are at the forefront in the national understanding of CBE. This journey in Rochester wouldn't have happened without the leadership of visionary district and school leaders. Erica Stofanak Pappalardo, Heidi Zollman, and Kathleen Cotton understand the heart, mind, and practice of educators. Kathleen was especially helpful during this past year as my writing coach. Erica's, Heidi's, and Kathleen's expertise, humor, strong work ethic, and common vision have been the accelerant to the fire lit by their former assistant superintendent, Mary Moriarty, and superintendent, Mike Hopkins. The eight-year journey toward CBE has spawned an amazing crew of teacher leaders who understand the strong framework needed in competency-based learning design. I am grateful for the trust and confidence they placed in my growing depth of understanding of CBE. We all came to appreciate products of our own learning while moving the Rochester School District forward. Coaching sessions with Mary Moriarty have always propelled me forward and have given me time for my own reflection on our work. Thank you, Mary. I am honored to work with you.

As a proponent of just-in-time learning myself, I am grateful and appreciative for all that I have learned in working with the outstanding team of school leaders and teachers at Sanborn Regional School District. My sincere thanks to Brian Blake, Ellen Hume-Howard, Brian Stack, Michael Turmelle, Ann Hadwen, Sandy Rutherford, Michael Shore, Jon Vander Els, Donna Johnson, Deb Bamforth, and Annie Rutherford. I continue to be inspired by their hard work and laser-like focus on student learning. I thank them for allowing me to walk this walk with them.

I am grateful to Barbara Munsey, retired superintendent of schools in Epping, for always advocating from the heart for her teachers and staff doing this monumental work of school transformation in a small school setting.

The Rochester, Sanborn Regional, Epping, Souhegan, Pittsfield, Concord, and other pioneering districts in New Hampshire's pilot accountability plan are embracing the multiyear commitment for their K–12 public systems founded on the principles of CBE. Although they are not yet at the move-on-when-ready model, they will be there soon as they continue the journey. They are dedicated to the ideals of CBE in shaping the national conversation on accountability at the federal level. I am grateful for the insight and skills of their school leaders and am appreciative of their patience and deliberation as I have coached and stretched thinking around this incredibly complex work.

Joe Crawford and Justin Krieger, the codirectors of the Next Charter School in Derry, represent two young, passionate leaders who, as assistant principals of their respective middle schools, designed Next to meet the needs of a certain profile of student who they knew would not be successful at the local high school. With those students in mind, Joe and Justin have embarked on a real journey to design Next as a competency-based high school focused on college and career readiness in a learning environment that is project-based in nature and non-course-based in design. I have been honored to work with them in their design footprint for Next.

Rob Lukasiak, a close associate in competency, assessment, and grading practice work for the past eight years, has always been helpful in talking through our thinking as we work school redesign projects. He is a mathematics specialist who understands performance assessment and the Common Core State Standards. His approach to performance indicators has really informed my thinking on where this all fits into unit design and course mapping. Rob and I have worked in many great school districts as we do this work.

Special thanks and appreciation for the many "voices from the field" who contributed their stories so that educators can better appreciate the nature of this work: Bryan Setser and Amy Swann of Matchbook Learning; Terry Bolduc, Ellen Hume-Howard, and Brian Stack of Sanborn Regional School District; Jon Vander Els of the New Hampshire Learning Initiate; Vincent Thur of Youth Connections Charter School; Danny Medved of the Denver School of Innovation and Sustainable Design; Monique Boudreau and Sarah Bond of Rochester School District; Bonnie Robinson of Lebanon High School; Kristin Wilson of the Fall Mountain School District; and Joe Crawford and Justin Krieger of the Next Charter School.

Special thanks to Nancy Walser of the Harvard Education Press, who encouraged me throughout the proposal development and writing process.

All the educators involved in CBE understand the compelling nature of this work. As we move forward, I know we will continue to use each other's expertise to inform our decisions along the many paths on this journey together.

About the Author

ROSE L. COLBY is currently a competency-based learning and assessment specialist, assisting schools in designing high-quality competency, assessment, and grading reform systems in many states. She is a Talent Cloud Fellow for 2Revolutions, an education design firm. She is a member of the national Advisory Board Company and a contributor to Competency Works, the national clearinghouse and resource for innovative practices in competency-based education. She has served as competency education consultant for the New Hampshire Department of Education for several years, providing outreach to New Hampshire schools districts in developing competency education as well as supporting districts in the development of the New Hampshire Performance Assessment for Competency Education (NH PACE).

Ms. Colby is a motivational speaker and presenter in the areas of competency-based learning, digital learning, differentiation, and school leadership. She has been a partner in the Nellie Mae Education Foundation–funded project centered on student success through extended learning opportunities in partnership with the QED Foundation, the nonprofit Plus Time NH, and the New Hampshire Department of Education.

Prior to 2006, Ms. Colby was the principal of Mountain View Middle School, which was awarded the New Hampshire Department of Education Excellence Award (School of the Year) in 1996 and 2001. While on sabbatical in 2002, she served as principal in residence for the Bill and Melinda Gates Foundation's New Hampshire School Administrators Leading with Technology project.

Ms. Colby currently teaches in the Educational Leadership Program at Plymouth State University. She is the recipient of the university's 2015 Dennise Maslakowski Memorial Award in Education.

Index